Patti

all th best

Andw Wood

What people are saying about
Cunningly Clever Marketing

"I love Andrew Wood's book. It made me laugh, wince, nod in agreement, howl, point out a statement to my wife, and become wiser in the ways of both marketing and reality. A superb read!"
> — **Jay Conrad Levinson, author, the** *Guerrilla Marketing* **series**

"Every auto dealership in the world should read this book; it's time to do things differently!"
> — **Mike Steventon, Head of Automotive Unit, KPMG, UK**

"I found the new and practical concepts in this book, BRILLIANT!"
> — **Alan Sutherland, CEO, Environmental Technologies**

"This is a must-read book for every business owner. To paraphrase Albert Einstein, it's insanity to keep doing the same marketing over and over again and expect to get different results. Yet, as the host of the radio program *New Construction Strategies,* my guests describe how their old marketing approaches are not working as their profit margins continue to decline. Fortunately, Andrew Wood's book, *Cunningly Clever Marketing,* provides a path for every business owner, including contractors, to shake up their marketing approach and increase their profits. Why do I recommend a competitor's product? Simply because it's that good.
> — **Ted Garrison, author,** *Strategic Marketing for Contractors*

"Andrew Wood understands what many marketing professionals fail to grasp: Marketing should produce a profitable response. You will enjoy his personal story and powerful insights into building a successful business through cunningly clever communications.
> — **Troy Waugh, author,** *Power Up Your Profits* **and**
> *101 Marketing Strategies*

"Short, to-the-point chapters focus on aggressive marketing that pays for itself. The author emphasizes building a list of prospects and hard-hitting, dramatic communication with them."
> — **Dan Janal, founder, PRleads.com; author,** *Dan Janal's*
> *Guide to Marketing on the Internet*

Cunningly Clever Marketing

The Inside Secrets
of a Marketing Legend

By Andrew Wood

SELECT PRESS

Legendary Marketing
www.LegendaryMarketing.com
800-827-1663

Published by Select Press
Novato, California
ISBN 978-189077-724-1

10 9 8 7 6 5 4 3 2 1

Printed in Korea

With many thanks to all the people whose books, tapes and seminars have shaped my thinking especially Brian Tracy, Jay Abraham, Dan Kennedy, Jay Conrad Levinson. and Rick Crandall.

Also to my Legendary Marketing staff whose job it is to execute all my crazy ideas!

Summary Contents

(A detailed Table of Contents follows on page ix.)

Detailed Contents

Introduction

Section 1

Section 3

Section 4

PRINT ADVERTISING THAT ACTUALLY WORKS

Section 5

TURNING YOUR WEBSITE INTO A
MONEY-MAKING MARKETING MACHINE   115

Section 6

Section 7

Section 8

Section 9

Section 10

MAXIMIZING YOUR PROFITS   275

Section 11

PERSONAL BRANDING   305

Section 12

NINJA MARKETING   327

Section 13

Section 14

INTRODUCTION

MUST READ
Very Important Introduction

Every Book Comes with Your Own Personal Marketing Vault of Additional Cunningly Clever Ideas!

This is no ordinary book. In fact, the pages of this book are just the beginning of your journey into the secret world of Cunningly Clever Marketing. Along with this book you get direct links to hundreds of additional samples, case histories, websites, and other priceless information.

The Cunningly Clever Marketing Vault gives you instant web access to audios, videos, ads, special reports, brochures, software — in fact, almost everything mentioned in this book is at your fingertips if you want to dig deeper into any strategy or concept discussed!

But that's all an additional priceless bonus — let's talk about this book!

In the following pages I'm going to share with you a lot of exciting ideas and concepts. I'm going to give you specific examples and case histories. I'm also going to tell you in detail about what works and what doesn't.

Best of all, I'll prove to you why something you have suspected for years is almost certainly true: Most of the money you spend on marketing is a disgusting waste of money!

Your current marketing is just not working the way it should!

In fact, it may not be working at all!

Websites are launched with almost none of the necessary back-end tools in place behind their flash façades to automatically increase business.

Direct mail is sent to people who have no interest in what you are selling.

Ads are run in publications that few people actually read.

Agencies are obsessed with "brand," "image," and "feel" because they don't understand how to actually make their marketing produce results. They would rather focus on THEIR abstract terms instead of YOUR revenue.

In this book I'm going to give you the inside secrets to squeezing every ounce of revenue from any marketing you ever undertake. Along the way I'm going to destroy a number of marketing myths and help you make the paradigm shift from the type of marketing most people think works to the type of marketing that will actually make you millions!

While the examples in the books are rooted in those businesses I know best, these ideas and techniques can be adopted, tweaked, and used to improve response in any business, in any country!

Let's get started...

Andrew Wood

P.S. A campaign is Not Cunningly CLEVER unless it increases leads and, ultimately, sales!

i1

The Critical
Paradigm Shift to
Cunningly Clever
Marketing

CHAPTER 1

Almost Everything I Learned About Marketing I Learned in a Karate School!

For a little more than 10 years, from the mid-Eighties to late Nineties, I was in the karate business. I built one small school in San Marcos, California into a national chain of 400 schools, starting with just $5,000 in cash and big dreams.

Along the way I learned some very important marketing lessons. The kind you only learn firsthand, when every single penny you spend comes out of your own pocket and has to produce results for you to survive!

Later I published my own magazine, owned a catalog company and advertising agency, and built a world-leading software company. While my knowledge of marketing increased rapidly along the way, I never forgot the lessons learned in that first small karate school.

Nor did I ever forget that the real goal of marketing is to produce income!

But allow me to share with you how my passion for marketing all started...

All I Ever Wanted to Be Was a Golf Pro!

But one small detail held me back from a career on the PGA Tour: lack of talent! I was good, but not nearly good enough.

Lack of talent held me back from a career in golf — but golf launched my career in marketing!

As fate would have it, my life-long love of cars paid off one dreamy afternoon as I waited to get off work. I sat on the bag rack outside the club-house in the balmy Florida air, having not seen a car for four hours. Suddenly I heard a loud whining noise and a silver 308 Ferrari screamed into view at the bottom of the driveway. Ignoring the posted speed limit by at least 40 mph, it quickly stopped in front of me. I took the clubs out of the passenger seat, the only place they would fit, and attached them to a golf cart.

The stocky, moustached owner got out and handed me a tip.

"Nice car!" I beamed.

"Yeah, thanks," he said and drove off to park.

As he walked back I bombarded him with questions about the car, all of which he gladly answered. Then he said, "Hey, kid, do you play golf?"

"Yeah," I said.

"Are you any good?" he asked.

"Yeah, I'm off scratch," I said.

"Think you can help me?"

"Sure!"

"Okay, what time do you get off?"

"3 pm," I said.

"Okay, I'll hit balls 'til then. Come meet me on the range when you're done because I suck; maybe you can help!"

As it turned the out, the man in the Ferrari was in the karate business and we swapped golf lessons for karate instruction. Soon after, I was accidentally thrust into a new career in the martial arts world.

My lifelong love of cars also contributed to my career change!

The Turning Point to Greatness

I bought my first school in San Marcos in 1986 from an older instructor who was moving to a larger town in an effort to grow his business. Not surprisingly, he failed.

Meanwhile, I turned his old school into a modest success in that I made enough money to make my car payment and pay the rent. However, I soon realized that whatever I was making was not enough, and so I did what everyone in the karate business does when faced with that situation: I opened another school!

In late 1987, I bought a second small karate school in Irvine, California with no money down from a doctor who had invested in the business and just wanted his name off the lease. The first month the business lost $1,000, the second month it lost $1,000, the third month it would have lost another $1,000 except I was already broke.

Sure, the phone rang occasionally or someone walked in with a coupon, but the weeks came and went with little real progress and zero profits.

Finally, one day in utter despair I sat down with a yellow pad and began some serious soul searching.

First, I asked myself what I was doing wrong.

Second, and perhaps most important, I wondered what I was going to do about it.

The simple act of writing questions down on paper can bring amazing clarity. I quickly realized (surprise, surprise) that the first thing I needed was paying customers. I also realized that my ads were not working, since the phone wasn't ringing.

Please understand what kind of Quantum Leap thinking was going on at this point. Most business owners or managers don't ever think like that when it comes to growing their businesses. Instead, they are far more likely to subscribe to the Professor Slutsky theory.

The Professor Slutsky Theory

For those of you not familiar with the good professor's work, allow me to digress a moment. The noted professor did pioneer work with frogs. He started his experiments with a perfectly good frog. He yelled *"jump"* until the frog moved and he then measured the leap.

Then, under anesthesia (in the most humane way possible), he amputated one of the frog's front legs and repeated the experiment.

After measuring again, he amputated the frog's other front leg, yelled "jump" and measured the leap, which as you can guess was decreasing. The frog's back left leg was cut off and again the professor yelled "jump." The frog's wobbly attempt was duly measured, whereupon the final leg was removed. The professor yelled "jump" once more but the frog did not respond. At which point, Professor Slutsky concluded that, "after amputation of all four legs ... the frog became deaf."

I mention this story because whenever marketing does not work, most business owners immediately point to the medium rather than the marketing itself. The newspaper doesn't work, TV doesn't work, radio doesn't work, and the web is just worthless hype! Rarely, if ever, do they consider the simple fact that their marketing SUCKS!

Eureka!

I came to that exact realization one October morning in 1987. What followed was a decision that changed my life forever.

After acknowledging that I didn't REALLY know the first thing about marketing, I rushed to the local bookstore and bought all *eight* of their marketing books. The first was David Ogilvy's classic, *Ogilvy on Advertising*.

I was amazed to learn how changing a simple headline could produce a 500% increase in response.

How adding a picture of scissors next to a coupon could increase redemption by up to 35%, how reverse type (white letters on black) sharply decreases readership, and so on.

The first advertising book I ever read — and still one of the best!

Before I finished the second book, I ordered *20 other books!* I was like a man possessed… highlighting, underlining, and taking notes for 30 straight days. All through the Christmas holiday I soaked up marketing information like a sponge.

After taking it all in and completely changing my approach (see advertising chapter), I designed some new ads to run the second week of January.

Bingo!

The phone rang off the hook. I signed up 30 new students in a single month, as opposed to the five I typically signed up! I was ecstatic, but realized there was still work to be done. If I could get such a massive increase in response just by studying the gurus of marketing, perhaps I could capitalize on these leads even more by improving my sales skills. I purchased tapes from the likes of Dale Carnegie, Tom Hopkins, Joe Girard, Zig Ziglar, and others. Suddenly, instead of closing two out of ten leads, I was closing eight out of ten and it didn't cost me a dime more to do it!

Next, I turned my attention to techniques like customer retention, newsletters, thank-you cards, and follow up. I adopted the tactics I found in books like Carl Sewall's *Customers for Life*. By the end of the year customers were staying an average of six months instead of three!

Imagine what it could do for your business if customers bought twice as much or stayed twice as long!

Nationwide Franchise from Scratch in Just Six Years!

At 27 years of age, my second year in business, I walked out of a 1250-square-foot karate school in a suburban strip mall with $128,000 in my pocket — a net gain of $121,000 over my previous year's income. Six years later, I had 125 franchise schools plus 275 affiliates nationwide and was making millions.

Lots of people built martial arts empires based on teaching styles or their fighting reputation. I did it solely on the RESULTS of my marketing system. I did it by creating a sales and marketing system that could be duplicated. Regardless of teaching style or location, a school owner could follow the blueprint and be guaranteed a predictable result for his time, money, and effort.

It's a system I have used in hundreds of businesses since and one whose foundations I am about to share with you.

There is no quicker way to grow your business than by improving the RESPONSE of your marketing.

A single Cunningly Clever campaign can vault your business to the very top of your industry!

CHAPTER 2

So What Do You Want to Sell Me?
Good Luck with That Marketing!

Do you want to sell me a house? A car? A vacation? A club membership? A new credit card? A funeral plot? Life insurance? Stocks? Whatever it is, I am, like you, on the "A" prospect list. People like you and me make a decent income and we are not afraid to part with a little money to buy things.

But — and it's a BIG BUT — most of the marketing we receive to entice us to part with our money is doomed to failure.

This week American Express/Delta sent me six letters (all the same letter) addressed to every company I have ever owned,

two of which I dissolved a decade ago! I left all of the letters out on the dinning room table to take a picture of them, which I was going to use to illustrate waste and poor mailing list quality — especially interesting since American Express sells their mailing lists!

Unfortunately, my wife, who has a cleaning fetish, threw them away. She thought they were junk mail "since they were all the same letter!"

I need not have worried, the following week all six letters showed up in the mail again.

What does it say about a company that has such incredibly wasteful marketing practices? I mean, the odd duplicate is acceptable, even expected, but a dozen letters in a week!

You're killing trees, people!

How about the $50 coffee-table book and boxed writing set that a North Carolina real estate development, The Cliffs, over-nighted to my 14-year-old son as "sales material" after he visited their website and requested more info? A beautiful package full of photographs that told you absolutely nothing useful about the land or homes they were attempting to sell to a 14-year-old with five hundred bucks in the bank (which is not likely to stay there beyond the next version of Xbox!)

Or Porsche of North America who sent me a $100 sales kit for their new turbo rather than a simple letter offering me, an existing customer, the first test drive when the new model arrived in my local showroom. I sold the sales kit on e-bay for $48 and bought a different car when the leasing department told me I had to pay the same rate I had paid the first three years (although the car was now half its original value) if I wanted to continue to own the car. Or I could drive 150 miles to the dealer and negotiate new terms!!

A high-end resort sends me an e-mail offer in 5-point type. I can read it but I know for a fact that 55% of people over forty can't, so they won't! I also know most of their prime customers are in their 50s! Amazing, but typical of many high-end resorts. Some 23-year-old web-graphics guy thinks big text looks uncool so he uses small-type text. No one thinks to actually check this "small" but important fact and so the email offer is doomed to deletion before it's ever read. If you look at the resort's website, you will see the trend continued! Nice, neat, and un-readable to well over 55% of their potential customers.

Nike, after a brilliant long-copy campaign a few years ago, just ran a series of two-page ads in 8-point reverse type (white type on a black background). It looks way cool, **only it's so small you can't actually read it!**

All of these examples are current, insane, and true. Big companies, small companies, and probably your company waste untold fortunes on ineffective marketing.

Just because a company is **BIG or well known does NOT mean their marketing works** (that is, produces leads and sales) and certainly does not mean their marketing is worth emulating.

Most large companies have TERRIBLE MARKETING!

Don't copy them!

CHAPTER 3

David and Goliath — Millions in Sales on a Shoestring!

At the same time as most organizations waste billions on ineffective marketing, others turn small budgets into Cunningly Clever results. Take Garland, the Michigan Resort that this year generated 1.7 million dollars in sales from just over 1,100 plain old *sales* letters, without discounting anything, in perhaps the worst economy in the United States of our lifetime! That figure does not include the onsite spending of those booking, so in reality you are looking at over two million dollars in sales from a campaign that cost just $20,000!

Or take the start-up franchise that grew from one location to over 150 franchisees in just 24 months with a relentless direct mail campaign aimed only at a hand-picked list of 197 opinion leaders in the industry!

How about the daily-fee golf club that built an opt-in email list of 60,000 golfers in just nine months using an insane idea. They simply offered free golf at the beginning and end of their season — two months when they never made any money anyway!

Or the business-to-business website run from a garage that was making $15,000 a month its third month in business, with a start-up cost of just $6,000. Their secret was a collaboration that got them access to 15,000 business owners in their industry for free! Now there's a dot-com success story!

How about a struggling consulting business that, instead of discounting, tripled its price and quadruped its business in just three months.

Imagine a single-page sales letter that starts by questioning the reader's sanity. That's made millions in numerous different industries!

Insulting and insane, but immensely profitable!

Just because **a company is small or has out-of-the-box ideas** that you might THINK are from another planet **does not mean they will not produce spectacular results!**

Most Cunningly Clever marketing does not look like everybody else's marketing!

CHAPTER 4

The 20 Top Reasons Why Most Marketing Fails!

In the TWO minutes or so you will spend reading the next few pages, I am going to save you hundreds of thousands of dollars and years of trial and error by detailing exactly why most businesses fail to reach their marketing goals. This is not subjective; this is not my opinion; it is based on over 20 years of research into the science of marketing and the analysis of several hundred clients.

Here are the 20 top reasons why businesses fail at marketing. **Read them, believe them, and resolve not to do them!**

1. **They don't collect enough leads or prospect data** because most of their marketing is NOT focused on lead generation.

2. **They don't do enough with the data** they do collect to convert leads to sales.

3. **Their websites are ineffective** because they are not set up effectively to collect, sort, and follow up on large numbers of leads.

4. **They do not track their campaigns** so they have no exact way of knowing which ads or promotions were really effective and which bombed.

5. **Their ads stink!** They have cute headlines, pretty pictures, *impotent* copy, and *insipid* offers that all conspire to eliminate any meaningful response.

6. They run marketing campaigns that their "people" like the looks of **rather than ones that actually get the phone to ring.**

7. There is **no written sales process** or scripting or training of the people answering the phone. This is the frontline of all sales success.

8. **Follow up to all requests is not automated** or systemized, so follow up on leads is poor.

9. They do almost **the exact same marketing** as ALL their competitors. They are afraid to take a risk.

10. Brochures, ads, and letters are **written in boring, generic corporate-speak** and wouldn't motivate a drunk to leave his seat for a free beer.

11. Their **budgets are based on a percentage of gross** or a number someone handed down from head office instead of being based on the goals they are trying to reach. In other words, the budgets are pure fantasy with no connection whatsoever to the income needed.

12. They **discount to get more business**, rather than look for ways to add more value.

13. They do NOTHING to **set themselves CLEARLY apart** from others in their marketplace. But still they say "We have the best customer service" (yeah, yeah, yeah, tell it to the judge — as my kids would say)!

14. Their **service is really about 80% worse than they think it is!** They have no system in place for measuring service so they never really know how good or BAD their service TRULY is!

15. They **fail to thank their customers** with letters, cards, and small gifts.

16. They confuse **loyalty programs** with **discount programs**! Loyalty is earned, NOT BOUGHT!

17. They **fail to outsource the things they don't do well** — like telemarketing, web marketing, and sales training.

18. They **don't capitalize on the automation** that's available to help them maximize their operations.

19. They **don't spend enough time studying or doing marketing.** You tend to get best the best results from the things you focus on the most!

20. They **keep doing what they have always done** because it's easier than changing to a more systematic approach that would actually work. Meanwhile, their marketshare is sinking faster than an elephant in quicksand.

Now you have the key information why most businesses don't get where they want to go. I'll tell you more about each of these topics later. For now, just accept them as gospel.

DO NOT make any of the above mistakes if you truly want to maximize your marketing.

CHAPTER 5

Mastering the Paradigm Shift from the Type of Marketing that People Expect You to Do to the Marketing that Actually Works!

Day in and day out my biggest challenge is convincing partners and would-be partners to make a radical and fundamental change in their thinking towards marketing ["partners" is how I refer to and think of my clients; see Chapter 20]. I want them to break twenty or thirty years of tradition and the bad habit of doing whatever everyone else does and make the switch to a more effective direct-marketing methodology.

Even when businesses cross the chasm and embrace the **Cunningly Clever Marketing Methodology**, all it usually takes is one ad from their competitors in a regional magazine to fire up ALL the staff naysayers.

"LOOK, OUR COMPETITION IS ADVERTSIING IN...[take your pick...the local newspaper, regional magazine, trade rag, or style magazine]...and we sit by and do NOTHING!"

"THEY ARE GETTING all our business!" cry the staff and the marketing lady!

"You cancelled all our ads!" they say, pointing at me.

"You are KILLING OUR BUSINESS!"

"The sky is falling!!!"

When this happens, as it frequently does, I ask a simple question. "Did you run ads in all these places last year?"

"YES!" they cry in unison!

"Did you also lose $500,000 last year?"

"Well, yes," they say in muffled voices as they look uncomfortably around the room at each other.

"Then...WHY do it again?"

"But," they always say, "look what our competition is doing!"

Yes, look, at what they are doing — blowing thousands of dollars on ads they aren't tracking and that don't work! Running direct-mail campaigns in reverse type that no one can read. Distracting people with their fancy flash website while failing to collect any data!

They are spending their way towards oblivion while you, my friend, are building the largest database of prospective customers of any business in the state. A database of real people who buy the products and services YOU sell.

In the process of building this huge prospect database you will drive more business by accident than your competitors do on purpose. Not only will you drive more business, but you will also have a huge database of people who have identified themselves as potential customers who you can now contact for almost nothing though email, and at an acceptable cost through highly targeted direct mail.

Until you have a database of qualified prospects large enough that selling 20% of them allows you to easily reach your goal, you should spend not one dime on anything but growing your database.

Make the critical paradigm shift from traditional advertising and marketing to database-driven direct-response marketing and find the marketing tools to effectively build your prospect lists!

If targeted, direct-response driven marketing does not work for your business then I can guarantee that neither will print, radio, TV, or billboards!

CHAPTER 6

Why He with the
Biggest Database Always Wins!

Like it or not, the title of this chapter is a fact!

This is a fact most business owners are not really very happy about since the total sum of their data collection efforts over the last 20 years amounts to 750 names and addresses and the 113 emails they collected this year but haven't yet gotten into the computer!

This may not be you but — trust me on this — I talk to hundreds of business owners a month and this example is better than average!

The size and quality of your database is your foundation for the long-term success of any marketing campaign yet the simplicity of this fact is lost on many. When I ask seminar audiences full of business owners and marketing executives what's the first thing they would do to market a new business, buying a database of people who have an interest in that product is rarely, if ever, mentioned. When it is, it comes way down the list of suggestions after running ads, going to trade shows, and even renting billboards.

A Tale of Two Corvette Stores

Imagine two businesses in Los Angeles that sell parts and accessories for Corvette sports cars. One has a database of 600 Corvette owners while the other has a database of 6,000.

Who do you think is in the position of strength?

One can market to a large enough database to maintain a healthy business while the other must run his business while constantly searching for more prospects.

It does not matter what business you are in. **You need a large enough database of people who have put their hands up as qualified prospects** so you can sort through them to find an adequate number of actual customers.

Most businesses do a terrible job of building their databases. Golf courses that have seen 50,000 people a year play their course for two decades have email lists that total 750 names (honestly, that's the average!).

Car dealerships selling hundreds of cars a month can't find 1,000 good addresses to mail to.

Local electrical, air conditioning, water purification, and lawn services do hundreds of transactions but never collect data on their customers. They are forced instead to run endless coupon ads looking for new customers when everyone they ever needed was already in their grasp!

If you are selling coffins, build a list of very old people. If you are selling video games, build a list of teenagers and young adults. If you are selling homes in Florida, build a list of affluent people who are about to retire. If you sell cigars, build a list of people who smoke them. If you sell stuff for weddings, build a list of people about to get married.

NOTHING is more important than building your database!

He with the biggest database of prospects wins!

Not occasionally, not some of the time, but *all* of the time, *every* time!

CHAPTER 7

There Are Only Three Ways to Grow a Business…Any Business!

Most people overcomplicate marketing with talk of image, brand, feel, look, style, and culture. These are all important, relevant factors — if you are a multinational company — and all are of of *little importance* if you are not!

What is important is the simple fact that there are only three ways to grow your business.

1. **Increase the number of clients.** This is where most businesses focus their effort, although it's very often the hardest of the three ways to increase income.

Large growth in number of clients usually comes from a change in pricing or a change in marketing focus.

When we changed one partner's prime marketing media from print advertising to targeted direct mail, we were able to add over half a million dollars in income the second year and over a million the third — with a small decrease in spending!

2. **Increase the average transaction value.** How can you get them to buy more of what you sell each time they call, visit, or click?

If ten people stand at the counter to buy a widget for $15, the 80/20 rule says that if all where offered the chance to buy six widgets for, say, the price of five, two people would do it, increasing your transactional value by over 53%!

Simple, but most customers rarely receive the offer. While the person is standing in front of them, daily-fee golf clubs sell one round instead of five. Shoe stores don't add socks or polish to a sale. Hotels sell that night's stay in the summer without trying to sell a return stay in the fall, and so it goes. There's no cost other than the few moments of time to make the offer:

> *Mr. and Mrs. Jones, have you ever had the plea-sure of being up here in Vermont when the leaves are changing? It's stunningly beautiful. Our fall packages just came out this week but they sell out very fast. Shall I go ahead and reserve yours while you are here today?*

3. **Increase the frequency of repurchase (or the length of time they stay as a customer).** How do you get them to buy more often to get more residual value out of each client?

I helped a software company massively increase its income by simply changing to a residual pricing model. Instead of charging $4,000 plus a small annual fee for maintenance, they now charge a set up fee of $1,500 and a $400 a month license fee. Since their average customer stays seven to ten years, you do the math! A simple change of marketing strategy that turned a struggling business into an extremely profitable enterprise.

There are a thousand things you can do in the name of marketing. Focus on exploring these three, in detail, first!

CHAPTER 8

Preach to the Choir — Don't Try to Covert the Muslims

Converting people from one set of values, beliefs, or vendors is a difficult, tiresome, expensive, and often dangerous or thankless task.

My first how-to manual sold a whopping 1,148 copies in its first year. Which at $150 each in an industry of 12,000 or so people was not half bad. Over the next decade I came out with over 50 additional products or services and for years I marketed them to the list of 12,000 business owners I had in that industry.

Never, not even by accident, did the 10,852 people who did not buy my first manual ever come close to reaching the sales of the 1148 people who did!

Eventually I resigned myself to the fact that, like it or not, my market in an industry of 12,000 business owners was in fact 1,148 people.

It took me years to reach this conclusion and tens of thousands of dollars in wasted printing, mailing, and postage. Once I stopped trying to convert more customers and instead started to focus on what other products and services I could sell to my existing customers, I was able to quadruple the size of the company in a matter of months!

Focus your effort first on existing customers, then on prospects, then on prospecting.

The first will always out-produce the other two!

2

Your USP: Powerful Positioning

CHAPTER 9

Businesses Unclear on the Concept

Do you really know what business you're in? Sounds simple, but very often I find that business owners think they are in one business while the customers think it's another business. For example, in the karate business, where 80% of the students are under 12, most instructors mistakenly believe that they are in the business of teaching karate or self-defense.

Ask any of the parents of these children why they signed their child up for lessons and one, perhaps two at the most, will say for karate or self-defense. The real reason parents sign their children up for karate is to help them gain self-discipline, focus, and concentration, to improve their grades in school, and to develop the traits of confidence and positive self-esteem. Having done extensive research into this particular market, I can tell you unequivocally that karate is rarely even mentioned in the top ten reasons.

Despite this fact, the great majority of instructors still fail to maximize their marketing efforts. They continue to advertise karate, the business they think they are in, while the customer continues to buy self-improvement for their children. Those schools that realize this, and change the focus of their marketing to self-improvement through karate, may teach the same physical curriculum as those who believe they are in the karate business, but they can expect to enjoy three to four times the response from their marketing efforts.

This poster for karate lessons focused on what parents are actually hoping to buy.

As Charles Revlon once said, "In the factory we make perfume, in the stores we sell hope!"

Remember, people buy for *their* reasons, not yours! You might brew the best coffee in town, but if everyone is coming to you for your donuts it would be better to focus your marketing message on donuts. It doesn't matter if you own a coffee plantation and grow the beans yourself — if your customers are coming for the donuts, it will pay you to go with the flow.

Forget what you are trying to sell and focus instead on what your customers are buying!

CHAPTER 10

Claiming Your Unique Selling Proposition Before Someone Else Does!

The term Unique Selling Proposition (USP) was first described more than 50 years ago in *Reality in Advertising,* the classic book by Rosser Reeves. While given much lip service, the concept of USP is seldom understood or executed well. Reeves said that your USP must meet three criteria to be complete and powerful:

- It must say to your consumer, "Buy this and you will receive this specific benefit."

- Your USP must be one that your competition does not, or cannot, offer.

- It must be strong enough to attract new customers to you.

Your USP is the foundation for your marketing and advertising efforts. It is your unique advantage you use to sell your business. Your USP should be so strong and memorable that it will both distinguish you from your competitors and attract new business. It should also be memorable enough to generate word of mouth to drive referrals.

Most businesses don't have a USP and therefore they never build a strong marketing program on a secure foundation. Instead they bounce from idea to idea and don't portray a consistent theme! In fact, I've had new partners who have proudly shown me the twenty different ads they had run over the last five years — each touting something different! This approach wastes lots of time, lots of money, and a great deal of effort!

What Comes to Mind When You Hear Domino's Pizza?

"Domino's delivers in 30 minutes or less or your pizza is free." That was Domino's unique selling proposition and it fueled one of the most rapid business success stories ever. Domino's wasn't really selling pizza — what they were selling was fast delivery. There are hundreds of different chains around the country that sell pizza. But when you think of Domino's, you think: Domino's delivers in 30 minutes or less. You might be interested to know that the ads with the 30-minutes-or-less guarantee haven't run in over two decades (ever since a driver was killed trying to get his pizza delivered on time). Yet the 30-minutes-or-less perception remains!

The same is true in the shipping business. There's UPS, the US Postal Service, Airborne Express, and a host of other services that claim to get your package delivered directly to your customer, across the country, overnight. But when you absolutely, positively, must have it there overnight, who would you use? If you said the Post Office, move to the back of the class! (They lose 100,000 packages a day!)

If you absolutely, positively, must have it there overnight, the only company to use is FedEx. That perception has survived even through their name change from Federal Express. They have a legendary reputation for fast and reliable delivery and practically own the word "overnight." You must do the same — own a concept in your market that defines what your business is all about. This will attract people to you like a magnet!

What benefit or word does your business want to own in the minds of your customers?

CHAPTER 11

Digging Deep for the
Difference that Matters

What is unique, truly unique, about your business, unique enough amidst the common clutter of shared features and benefits **to get me to spend my money with you?**

Let's switch gears for a moment and get you thinking in another direction about this very same topic. Within a given price range, what's the difference between one hotel and another?

Not much! But sometimes even something small is enough to influence a person's purchasing decision. I now try to book my stays at Westin hotels not because they are particularly better in any respect from other higher-end hotels, but they do offer and MARKET very cozy beds. They call them "heavenly beds," but whatever they call them, I can tell you this: It's the closest thing to sleeping in my own bed when I am on the road. What's more, I'm willing to travel a little further out of my way and pay a little more to get it! At a lower price point and for, say, driving cross country, I would choose Wingate Inns because I KNOW they will have working high-speed Internet access, for free! It astonishes me that ALL hotels these days don't, but they don't, so why get stuck?

There is another hotel chain that struck a deal with the NBA by buying longer beds!

Motel Six is the clear leader in the perception of cheap!

At Holiday Inn kids stay and eat free!

These all are simple yet potent examples of positioning yourself as better and different in an incredibly crowded market!

So what ONE Unique SELLING Proposition (USP) are you going to build on and CHAMPION in your marketplace?

All it takes is ONE, but without it you are just another business saying how good your service is...and they all do that!

CHAPTER 12

Avoiding the Muddle in the Middle

In every market there is a Ferrari and a Yugo, a Rolex and a Timex, a Ritz Carlton and a Motel 6, a Neiman Marcus and a WalMart. The closer you are to the top or the bottom of your market, the easier it is to meet expectations and to price your product or service correctly to maximize profits.

The problem is that most companies find themselves drawn to the middle of the market. This muddled area is where they are neither the best nor the worst, the most expensive nor the cheapest, the newest nor the oldest, the quickest nor the slowest.

The middle of the market is by far the most difficult area in which to compete. You should first try to move towards one end or the other by either increasing your service and offerings to increase your price, or by decreasing service and offerings to lower prices and increase volume.

In my experience, the latter is actually the harder of the two to accomplish successfully. In contrast, it's relatively easy to add something that moves you up and differentiates you in the marketplace:

- the hair salon that greets you with a glass of champagne while you wait

- the gym that has video games built into the rowing or cycling machines so you compete on-screen in a simulated race against others

- the bar with a plateful of trendy appetizers (to offset the even trendier prices) that is delivered just as your first drink is almost gone so you stay for a second drink as you eat the food

- the only parking lot in town that offers a free car wash

- you create a new category — a category that you can lead

Take yourself out of the muddle in the middle by doing something different that allows you to be a leader in your own category. The only business in your category that also offers X — where X is a strong enough factor to create a new, or at least stronger, position within your category.

CHAPTER 13

Southpaw Marketing

In the Nineties, the Japanese company Yonex had a little run with a graphite-headed golf club that was selling well. They also had one other thing going for them: They signed one of the PGA Tour's most popular players and the world's undisputed best left-handed golfer, Phil Mickelson.

I spent almost a year trying to convince them that their USP should be *"The world's best left-handed golf clubs."* Statistically 10% of the 27 million people who play golf are left handed. No one in the world had ever claimed to be the world's best left-handed golf clubs, so the position was OPEN!

HELLO!

AN OPEN UNIQUE SELLING PROPOSITION in this over-crowded marketing world!!!

This was, and still, is a serious marketing opportunity!!!

But the wise people of Yonex thought that .000000001% or whatever they have of the right-handed market was better than total DOMINATION of the left-handed market!! They just couldn't see pigeonholing their market like that!!!

Why be the undisputed leader in a US market of 3 million left-handers, and a worldwide market of 30 million or so, when instead you can be a nobody in the worldwide market of 150 million right-handers? HELLO!!!

You will eat better being a big fish in a small pond!

CHAPTER 14

What's in a Name?

Choosing the right business or product name is an area that is very touchy for many people. That's because the chances are that you already have a good deal invested in a name. You might like the name you have. You have almost certainly invested in business cards, stationery, and signs. You might have been in business in your town or industry for a great many years using this name. You might feel that no matter what else you might change, you just have to stick with the name you already have.

You don't!

In fact, not changing your name may handicap you from ever achieving a big goal at all!

While a bad name can forever put you behind the eight ball, a good name, a simple name, a catchy name, can play a huge part in building your reputation quickly. So can aligning your name with existing perceptions. Yet human nature being what it is, most people will go to their graves defending a name they have already taken rather than making a simple change that can have a huge impact on their businesses.

The same goes for the name of your product or service. The name can be critical to your success. It's hard, if not impossible, to build a legendary reputation on the back of a lousy name. Despite this fact, many companies, big and small, soldier on, handicapped with a bad name because they feel they cannot change it!

Sometimes when you move on in business, or introduce new products, the name you started with is not a very accurate way to describe what you do now.

When I started out in business and didn't know any better, I used the generic name Andrews International. As my karate consulting business grew and more and more people entered the my consulting market — a market I practically created — I saw that some of them were better positioned than I was just because of their names. Immediately upon realizing this, I changed the company name to The Martial Arts Business Association. That was a much more descriptive and accurate definition of what we did. We offered seminars, consulting, a trade show, an industry magazine, and various publications. The name implied that this would be the case, whereas Andrews International needed a lot of explaining.

I frequently advise partners to change their business names and logos to something that is more interesting, something that stands out, something that gives them a clear edge, something that people want to buy!

Yes, you can change your business name or product name! Pick a name that highlights your benefits and attracts people to you.

CHAPTER 15

The Awesome Advantage of Cunningly Clever Names

Let's consider some Cunningly Clever business names. Die-hard batteries has a great brand name that in effect describes what you want the product to do — last a long time and never let you down late at night in a dark parking lot! It needs no explanation and therefore no marketing money need be wasted on explaining the product. Instead it can be spent on selling the product! (J.C. Penney had a similar battery at the same time that went nowhere because of a weak name.)

Supercuts hair franchise also has a nice descriptive name that focuses on results. Sears' line of tools has a great name: Craftsman. Toys "R" Us is a great name for a business that offers the largest selection of toys. Because it's a great name, it has been widely copied by others like Babies "R" Us, Pets "R" Us, and so forth, and, for the most part, the concept probably works — the perception being that you will have a large selection of a specialized product.

With their unusual names, Ugly Duckling and Rent-a-Wreck carved out a nice niche at the bottom end of the rental car market.

Because you probably don't have the massive financial resources of the big players in your town or industry, you must take great care in deciding on your business name. Over time, it will be your most potent weapon in conquering your market. Your name should capitalize on your key strength, the one thing you have that others don't, or even if they do have it, the thing they are not claiming (your USP).

For example, Toys "R" Us may stock hundreds of model trains, but that's not their specialty. They stake their reputation on having a huge general selection at low prices. That would allow you to enter the model train business and claim the position of model train specialist with a name like **Casey Jones Model Trains.**

This name positions your store as one for the collector or serious hobbyist. It states clearly that you are an expert on the subject and that people could come to you and get questions answered by a professional. This is brought about by the name "Casey Jones," immortalized in song, print, and television as perhaps the world's only legendary train engineer. People into trains will get the connection, even if others may not!

The most effective business or product names are the ones that connect instantly with your customers' needs.

CHAPTER 16

Put the Benefit to the Customer in Your Business or Product Name

When considering a new name for your company, unless you have untold millions to spend, pick a name that describes what you do in a way that people will understand. For example, all things being equal, if you had a computer problem, turned to the online Yellow Pages, and had the choice of calling:

- Jack Brown & Associates,

- AAA Computers, or

- The Computer Doctor

who would you call first? Ninety percent of people would call The Computer Doctor because the name suggests expertise and an immediate solution to their problem.

Let's say you are new in town and your young child has a toothache. Would you call Bob Talbot, Dentist or The Bright Smiles Family Dental Clinic? You need a number of repairs done around the house, would you call Mr. Fixit or Joe Smith & Sons?

Political fund-raisers always use a nice-sounding name for their cause because a nice-sounding name gets a better response. Concerned Citizens Against Higher Taxes sounds a whole lot more appealing than the Big Tobacco Companies Against a Five Cent Increase in the Tobacco Tax!

Everyone knows you ought to put a benefit in ad headlines. Why not go one step further and put the benefit in your business or product name?!

CHAPTER 17

Leverage Existing Perceptions, Don't Fight Them!

Another way to create a good name is to leverage existing perceptions. When defining your reputation and working to find the right name, it pays to remember that you cannot create a legendary reputation by fighting preconceived perceptions. Instead, you must leverage off existing beliefs or create a new product or service not shaped by existing notions. For example, you can't be cheap and also high in prestige — people will just not buy the concept.

Lexus would never have enjoyed the success they have in the marketplace if they had kept the name Toyota. Toyota means small, cheap, and reliable. Lexus now means prestige, quality, and reliability. Nissan did the same thing with Infiniti, spending millions on a new name because they knew that Nissan was not a name that people would associate with a high-priced, prestigious automobile.

But what if you have spent decades and invested billions in your name — can you really still change it? Take the Standard Oil Company. Their problem was that there were so many "Standard" companies that it created a great deal of confusion; the solution was to change their name to Esso, later Exxon — short, memorable and the only one! Similarly, in the Seventies Datsun changed their name from Datsun to Nissan.

A martial arts supply store in California made huge inroads on its competition by billing itself in the Yellow Pages as a Martial Arts Super Store. Despite the fact that it was smaller in size than the others in the area, it succeeded in part because of its claim. A business that calls itself a "super store" or "megastore" will be thought of as larger than its competitors. Similarly, any business with the name "warehouse," such as Book Warehouse, Liquor Warehouse, or Plant Warehouse automatically suggests a lot of products at low prices.

An Italian bistro sounds warmer and friendlier than an Italian restaurant. A boutique sounds much more upscale than a clothing store. A car doctor sounds like someone who can do more than a mechanic, doesn't it?

By taking words such as warehouse, boutique, or doctor and applying them to your business, you create a certain preconceived idea about your company that can jump-start your reputation.

Your name can either give you a huge edge or send you into oblivion. No matter how much time or money you have invested in your name, if it's bad, if it's nebulous, if it doesn't stand out from the crowd and give your reputation an edge, change it!

Your industry, city, or customer has preconceived notions about the business or service you offer. How can you align your business or product name with these notions to gain a competitive edge?

CHAPTER 18

Keep It Simple

When Apple Computer started out, their name would not fit into any of the previously mentioned categories. They did, however, have two big advantages.

- First, their market, personal computers, was a brand new market.

- Second, their competition had really terrible names. Which name would you remember: the MITS Altair 8800, The Commodore Pet, the IMSAI, or the Apple? Not exactly rocket science is it to conclude that those other companies spent millions trying to build a reputation for faulty names!

Legendary Marketing is a name that says success.

Ping Golf Clubs won big with its name by keeping it simple, and naming their product after the sound made when their early putters hit the ball squarely! Now that's genius: Every time a player used their product, it said their name — PING!

I wish I'd thought of that!

Keep it simple and make it easy to remember!

CHAPTER 19

Cunningly Clever Logos

It astonishes me how much money companies will spend on logos and just how bad most of them are! Remember the Lucent Technologies million-dollar circle that looked like the stain from a coffee cup?

Which name and logo do you think sold more apparel: Hunters Pointe Golf Club or Loch Ness Links?

Now that wasn't rocket science, was it? A simple change that exploited the fame of Loch Ness opened up hundreds more possibilities for Cunningly Clever marketing. It did not hurt either that the course and clubhouse had a very Scottish-links-style feel and a giant lake in front of the clubhouse.

The San Jose Sharks were for the longest time the best-selling logo in the NHL. I am sure my team the Tampa Bay Buccaneers quadrupled their apparel sales when they dropped the old fashioned buccaneer in favor of a much cooler pirate-style skull-and-crossbones logo.

I have three simple rules for designing logos:

1. Unless you have unlimited funds try and make the logo a pictorial representation of what you do (for example, a hammer squashing a bug for pest control).

2. Try to make it appealing enough that people — your employees and customers — would want

to actually wear it on their shirts (thus, in the bug example, it would probably have to be humorous).

3. Use colors and type styles that are easy to read and make sense in your industry. Failing that, stand out by using colors that no one in your industry currently uses!

You can change your logo!

And you don't have to spend a fortune with fancy design firms to come up with a winner.

CHAPTER 20

Does Your Business Have Customers, Clients, or Partners?

Disney has guests, not customers. The Masters golf tournament has patrons, not crowds, and I have partners, not clients (in case you wondered why I used that term earlier).

What difference does it make what you call the people who pay your bills?

Quite a lot, actually!

It makes a difference how your employees react to service requests.

It makes a difference how both parties THINK about the relationship.

Partners help get you business.

Partners ask for advice.

Partners also accept some highs and lows in a relationship.

For a partner you will leverage other relationships and assets to their advantage.

I go out of my way to correct partners who refer to themselves as customers or clients and I feel it really does make a difference.

Positioning is not just about how the outside world sees your business, it's also the core of how you and your employees see yourself and do business.

3

The Art of

Optimum Pricing

CHAPTER 21

How to Double Your Profits Overnight!

Optimum pricing is quite simply the quickest and easiest road to marketing success, yet it's very often the least-used and least-tested strategy.

This is because optimum pricing often means raising prices and this raises the FEAR FACTOR!

After all, if you don't have enough business now, how can you possibly get more business by increasing what you charge? It's an argument that seems to be based in solid logic yet, time and time again, this logic is proved to be wrong when actually tested!

Ask three business owners how they determine their pricing and you'll get one of these three answers:

- We price based on the competition
- We price based on a percentage over cost
- We price based on what we "FEEL" the market will bear!

Here's what you won't hear:

We have tested our pricing and it's the optimum combination of volume and price!

or

We price based on the amount of profit we want to make in relation to the amount of effort we want to expend.

What's the difference between a $100 an hour dentist and a $200 an hour dentist? A $50 watch and a $150 watch? A $300-an-hour attorney and a $400-an-hour attorney? In almost every case, it's not about quality — the difference is about 100 bucks!

When doing seminars for golf teaching professionals, I always ask what they charge for a one hour lesson. Usually this ranges from $40 to $150 and everywhere in between. So I take the first guy who charges $40 and the first one who charges $80 and ask the $40 person if the other pro is, in fact, twice as good at teaching as he or she is.

They never say YES!

It's the same with every other type of business, profession, or product I deal with. In almost every case the guys who get more for their product or service are simply the guys who decide to charge more!

Why many people will pay more is a chapter or three in itself. Some of the reasons are that people don't care about a few dollars more, they like you, you're convenient, or they think you're better if you charge more!

Everyone thinks their market is different. Everyone thinks their economy is worse, their customers cheaper, and their competition stiffer than anywhere else. Yet there is always someone in every market who charges far more than anyone else — and gets it!

Why not let that someone be you?

CHAPTER 22

The Millionaire, the Plumber, and the Dentist — Timeless Lessons in Value Pricing

There is the old story about the millionaire who wakes up in the middle of the night to find his toilet overflowing and water seeping down the hallway. He goes to the phone and calls the first plumber in the phone book who offers 24-hour service. Fifteen minutes later the plumber arrives and is escorted straight to the offending bathroom. After quickly surveying the scene, he grabs a large wrench from his tool kit and slams it down on top of the pipe just behind the overflowing unit. With that, a loud gurgling sound is emitted and the water quickly disappears down the pipe and returns to its original levels. The millionaire, amazed, thanks the man and asks for the bill. At once, the plumber says $500.

"That's outrageous," says the millionaire, "You just pulled that out of the air. All you did was hit that pipe with a wrench, and you have only been in the house two minutes. I want an itemized bill."

"Certainly," says the plumber, reaching into his overalls for a pen and scribbling on a tattered invoice.

Emergency plumbing service itemized bill

$5 for two minutes spent locating the pipe and hitting the pipe with a wrench.

$495 for the 20 years of training and experience that taught me where to hit it!

Total: $500

Another similar classic is the story of the dentist who is called in the middle of the night by a friend with serious toothache. Off he goes to his surgery in the small hours and proceeds to pull the offending tooth in just a few minutes.

The patient asks for the bill and is shocked when it comes to several hundred dollars. He indignantly protests saying, "Is this bill right? You only took two minutes to pull that tooth."

Smiling kindly the dentist replies, "Would you rather I had taken an hour?"

The moral of these stories, of course, is not to sell yourself short which, when it comes to pricing, most people do. Price for your experience, the value of your solutions, or your product's life expectancy, not for how long it takes you to do the job or how much it costs you to make the widget!

CHAPTER 23

The Most Profitable Expansion
I Never Made!

In 1988 my karate school was having a banner year with over 250 active students shuffling in and out of a 1,250 square foot dojo. It was busy, it was noisy, and there was barely enough room to teach classes. The parents were complaining, the students were complaining, and I was beginning to think it might cost me business if I did not expand.

One day out of the blue the landlord called me and told me the ice cream store next door was going out of business and asked me if I wanted to take over the lease. I immediately said yes as it seemed to answer all my problems. Fortunately, that night when I got home I started to think about it.

I was already paying $3,000 a month in rent, which, at that time, was twice what any other city in California was getting for the same space. If I took the new space it would jump to $6,000 a month, then of course I'd have to hire another instructor to teach, so in effect I'd be going backwards unless I could sign up an additional 100 plus students. I'd been in business long enough to know that reaching 250 was a milestone and that ALL of the schools I knew with more students than I had made about half as much money!

The next day I told the landlord I had reconsidered and did not want the space. Instead I immediately increased my rates by

50%. Here's the funny thing: It made absolutely no difference to my sign-up rates, it just made me twice as much money.

I should note that I gave all of my existing students the option to prepay at the existing rates, which many of them did.

Increasing volume is VERY OFTEN confused, even by smart people, with a better business. Instead of expanding your customer base and overhead, consider expanding your profits by simply raising the price!

CHAPTER 24

When the Customer Says No to Your Price — Double It!

In 1990, with the help of my good friend David Miller, I published my first book *How to Make $100,000 or More a Year Teaching Martial Arts.* The book was in binder form and was

We doubled the price of this manual and sold just as many copies as at the lower price.

374 pages. We decided to price the book at $79.95 since we had a very limited market. We asked a number of school owners if they would pay this for a book and they quickly said NO, but we decided to test it anyway. We did our first direct mail campaign to 12,000 schools. A whopping 4,000 envelopes came back as bad addresses, moved, or gone out of business, but we sold 100 copies to net a small profit from the first mailing.

Armed with a little confidence and a clean list, we almost doubled the price to $150 and mailed again, selling another 100 copies.

Twice the profit by simply doubling the price and yet when

we asked school owners if they would pay even the lower price, they had said NO!

That year we sold over 1,000 manuals at $150, bringing in $150,000. Had we kept the price at $79.95 and not tested a higher price, we would have made $75,000 less for the exact same information and effort!

What people say they will pay and what they WILL pay is often not the same thing.

You have to test to be sure!

CHAPTER 25

How an Ad in the *LA Times* for Motivational Guru Anthony Robbins Made Me $18,000 in Less Than a Minute!

A year or so later, I was in my school one day when the phone rang and the caller asked if I did seminars based on the information in my manual. At that very moment I was reading an ad in the *LA Times* for an Anthony Robbins business seminar. The motivational guru was doing a seminar in Anaheim and charging $600 a person, which back then sounded like an awful lot of money.

I told the caller I did do seminars and threw out the $600 figure for no other reason than that's what Anthony Robbins was charging for his seminar and I figured I knew a lot more about running a karate school than he did. The caller said fine and that he had others who wanted to come, what was the date of my next seminar? I quickly picked a date 12 weeks from then and, on the strength of this one guy's interest, decided to do a mailing.

I was astonished to find 40 people showed up — $24,000 for my FIRST ever speaking engagement! There is no way that at that time I'd have paid $600 to hear someone speak, but it didn't matter because there were 40 people who would and did. Would I have gotten any more people if I had said $300 instead of $600? I doubt it (and later tested prices as low as $99), but through dumb luck I made the decision to charge $600 and made an $18,000 profit in two days because of it!

Just because you wouldn't pay a specific price for a product or service does not mean others will not.

Repeat this to yourself several times a day!

CHAPTER 26

Make the Entry Easy — Then Upgrade

A key factor in pricing is the long-term value of your customer. When you get a customer to buy once it's much easier to get them to buy again and to buy more. For this reason it's worth looking at loss-leader pricing, but this will only pay off with a solid residual income or up-sell process in place!

When I started my software company, Marketing Commander, we offered our product with no set-up fee and no contract. This made it easy to attract our initial partners, although with each new partner we went further in the hole. As the product became more sophisticated and offered more benefits, we increased our prices and continued to build our residual income stream. Although we were not cheaper, most all of our competitors required up-front fees and contracts.

At Martial Arts America, we offered a free membership and no contracts. This was highly unusual at the time. You could sign up for four months for just $199 — but after six weeks we would go for a three-year black-belt program upgrade at $3,000.

Software companies are masters of the try it free, pay a residual fee, then upgrade to the deluxe model. It's a great model!

Cut up-front fees, cut paperwork, make doing business with your company painless, then upgrade them!

CHAPTER 27

Jay Abraham and the Dumbest-Ever Five-Million-Dollar Marketing Idea

By the mid-Nineties I had sold my first few karate schools and been in the karate consulting business for four years. I

had a series of how-to manuals, videotapes, seminars, a consulting service, and my own magazine, *Martial Arts Business*. I was traveling 60,000 miles a year and bringing in $30,000 a month from my garage. I had an expensive home in a gate-guarded community, a Porsche, a golf club membership, and my kids in private school. But the downside was, I wasn't making any profit!

This magazine helped position me as the top karate marketing guru, but I wasn't turning a profit.

I had $120,000 on my credit cards, had sucked all the equity from my home and burned through every dime I had made in my karate schools the first time around. I was about six weeks away from losing my home and going under because I was losing 10 grand a month!

At this time Jay Abraham was *the* big-name marketing guru. He ran huge seminars where people paid outlandish sums of money to attend while he charged $5,000 an hour for personal consulting. I had read all of Jay's books and listened to his tapes and was eager to meet him in person. This was eventually arranged by a friend who knew someone who knew Jay's wife. A short time later I was welcomed into Jay's huge Pacific Palisades home where, after the perfunctory greetings, we relocated to a small breakfast joint near his home.

My breakfast with Jay Abraham changed my fortunes.

There, for the next three hours, Jay grilled me about my business while poking me with his finger at every opportunity to drive home his points. How many clients do you have? How big is your database? How often do you mail them? What are your offers, and a million more questions delivered in machine-gun fashion.

After each answer he would make a suggestion or comment to which I would answer that I already do that or have tried that. As lunch drew to an end, he was getting increasingly frustrated, loud, and animated as I continued to assure him that I was doing or had tried all the suggestions he was giving me, many of which I had gleaned from his books and tapes.

Finally he got up and said, "You're so F-ing smart, figure it out for yourself," and marched out of the restaurant. My friend (who had arranged the meeting) and I sat at the table stunned, but before we had time to speak Jay came back and sat down.

"Look," he said, "I'm sorry. I'm sorry for wasting your time and even more sorry for wasting mine! Let's start again. How much money are you taking in each month?

"$30,000," I answered.

"And how much are you spending?" he said.

"$40,000," I answered.

"And how much do you want to make?"

"Well, if I could make $60,000 a month, life would be great!"

"Okay," he said, "that's easy. Just double your prices! Find something you can add to the program to increase the value and double the price." And with those words of wisdom he bid us goodbye and left!

On the long journey back down the 5 freeway we talked about the marketing guru's advice — or, in our opinion, total lack of advice. After all, it had taken us a long time to build the business up to the level it was at now. Even with my previous positive experience in testing and raising prices how could doubling our prices make it any easier?

With the wonderful LA traffic, it was nearly 5 pm by the time we neared home so we stopped off at Friday's Bar and Grill where a couple of other employees joined us for a few pints of Heineken. After the retelling of the story and at least three pints, one of the guys said, "Just imagine, if we did double the price, what could we put in the box to get them to pay twice as much?

At first the answers came slowly, but as the beer rolled on, so did the ideas, until in our inebriated states we thought we just might have a package of benefits that COULD work. At least we might be able to get 20 or so clients to pay more!

Two weeks later was our annual convention with 200 people in attendance, 100 of whom were on our monthly consulting program at $79.95 a month. (A price picked only because $7,995 was the combined cost of my mortgage, Porsche payment, and golf club dues.) The consulting consisted of a monthly package of ads, audios, videos, and promotions that they could use to grow their schools.

When I first started selling the product, all I had was a logo.

At the very end of the convention, armed with nothing more than a logo, I stood in front of the audience and told them about the **Masters Club.** This was essentially the same as the Hundred Club $79.95 monthly consulting program with a few more bells and whistles (like a monthly newsletter on disk they could customize for their clients, and a series of posters promoting the benefits of martial arts). At the end of my presentation I dropped the bomb, the new program would cost "just" $200 a month!

For about a minute there was total silence; suddenly a man at the back yelled out, "I want to be the first Mr. Wood. Your stuff has helped me so much I know it has to be worth it!" as he walked forward waving his checkbook. Another followed, then another, soon it was like a bible convention with people yelling out and jostling in line to sign up. 109 signed up that day and we still didn't have anything to actually show them.

By the time we shipped the first package six weeks later we had 200 people on board and had raised the price to $250 a month. 90 days after that on that back of a strong direct mail campaign we were approaching 400 customers. I had gone from making $30,000 a month and losing $10,000 to making over $100,000 and netting $60,000 in just three months! By Christmas I was totally out of debt and driving my first Ferrari!

Even now looking back on it, it seems incredible. It seems stupid. It seems like doubling your price and adding a couple of widgets would be just about the dumbest thing a business could do. BUT after struggling for several years, doubling our price quadrupled our business and turned a failing business into a five million dollar success!

Challenge your pricing logic; it just may be the easiest way to make money.

Adding one or two small things to your marketing package can reap huge rewards in increased pricing!

CHAPTER 28

Change the Experience — Triple Your Price!

Can you imagine buying a product on a regular basis for which the price you paid for the exact same product varied by as much as 800% on any given day?

Can you imaging charging your customers, say, 300% more than you do right now and getting them not only to accept it but to recommend you to all of their friends?

Can you imagine being the most expensive business in town and having people lining up at your door to get in?

If you buy a bottle of imported beer at a wholesale store, it will cost you about a buck. Buy the same beer at the local bar, and it will cost you about two dollars and fifty cents. If you buy the same beer at my country club, it will cost you four dollars, and if you buy the exact same beer at the bar of the hotel overlooking Central Park in New York City as I did only last week, you will pay a whopping eight dollars for the very same drink.

How much is this bottle of beer worth? It depends...

Since the beer is identical at all venues, why am I or anyone else willing to pay such a wide range of rates, a difference of 800% for the very same green bottle filled with 12 ounces of the identical liquid?

The answer is that we are all conditioned to put a premium on the experience more than the actual product itself. This is true today more than ever — consumers want an interactive experience. They want a taste of the good life, their own 15 minutes of fame or fantasy, and they are willing to pay highly for the experience.

Auto Week now lists over 50 places where for a couple of thousand bucks you can learn to drive like Jeff Gordon or Lewis Hamilton in real race cars. Talk about an experience for the average red-blooded male. For about the same price you can pilot a MIG fighter in mock combat or float across the Serengetti at sunset searching for wildebeests.

Back a little closer to home, you can take a very average business and double your income by increasing the experience. A hairdressing salon I used to visit in California used this very strategy to almost triple their prices. One day it was a regular unisex haircut place, the next it was a posh salon. The difference? Fancy tile on the floor, a new paint job, better-looking fixtures and a new name. But what really did it for me was the glass of champagne that magically appeared in my hand as soon as I walked in the door. I hardly noticed that the price of a haircut had tripled because I enjoyed the experience more than before!

I have also seen several examples of salons set up just for kids complete with horses or race cars to sit in while they are actually getting their haircut. Another had small TVs on the arm of each chair with popular cartoons playing. What's the betting they get a premium price for nothing more than a fancy chair and a couple of small TVs?

Change the focus from product to experience and you can charge whatever you like!

CHAPTER 29

Accomplishing the Million-Dollar Turnaround Two Bucks at a Time!

This year I started consulting with a Golf and Spa Resort located in a depressed area that had lost just under $1,000,000 last year. Astonishingly, in just 9 months in the worst economy in two decades we have turned it around. Obviously there are a lot of factors like cost savings and driving leads that go into such a radical turnaround but, by far, the most important is still pricing.

Because people come and go, many businesses are stuck with the pricing of the previous three chefs, the former marketing manager, or the boss's past girlfriend. **The last thing most new hires will do in any company is vigorously challenge pricing policy.**

BUT…

Why have a filet mignon on the menu that makes a $2 profit when pasta à la vodka makes $10?

Why charge the same for rooms on the busiest six weekends of the year when people will pay double on those particular dates?

Why not sell two rounds of golf instead of one? For example, $50 a round or $75 for as much golf as you want to play?

By challenge pricing at every level of the resort from a dinner salad to a full-day spa treatment, we were able to find an additional $500,000 in revenue, two or three dollars at a time. Coupled with cost cuts and increased traffic, this produced an astonishing turnaround.

When did you last challenge ALL of your pricing? Two dollars here and there can make a huge difference.

CHAPTER 30

Beating the Discounters by Changing the Game!

In every industry there are always some people who discount, discount, discount — usually to oblivion. The key when this happens is to simply change the game. Do not allow the customer to compare apples to apples. Instead change your offer to make the comparison apples to oranges.

Your gas is a few cents more, but you offer a free $10 automatic car wash!

If your gas station or coffee house was on an interstate, FREE Internet access would be a great reason to stop!

Your rental cars are not the cheapest, but you will pick up the customer for free! You know that if you don't have a car that's a big deal!

Your retirement homes are a little more than the community down the street, but you offer free golf for life!

Your apartments are $50 a month more than the complex next door, but you have a gym and a lower security deposit.

Your tires cost more, but you guarantee them longer.

Your lunch costs more, but you guarantee it on the table in 10 minutes or less so people can get back to work!

When facing discounting in your area, add something to change the customer's perception from cost to value!

CHAPTER 31

The Law of Three

On a recent visit to a chiropractor I was given a choice of seven different pricing plans. I took one adjustment and told him I would think about it.

I'm still thinking two months later!

A company bidding for my gardening offered five different plans depending on the level of service I wanted. I chose another company that offered two!

A golf club I consulted with in Tennessee had fourteen — count 'em — 14 different membership options!

Too many pricing options confuse your prospects. Confusion causes fear. Fear causes paralysis, not action!

Give customers options, but keep them simple and clear, in the only place that matters, their minds!

In the karate business, we offered three basic packages:

- a month-to-month no-frills program

- a four-month program that included a free uniform and belt, or

- our three-year black-belt-club program with a special uniform, patch, card, plaque, extra classes, and private instruction.

People would typically sign up for the middle program as it offered the most value but without a long-term commitment. This way they could try out the lessons for a while. Then within a matter of four to six weeks almost everyone would step up to the black-belt club. The choices were very clear and obvious.

We sell Marketing Commander in three packages. I advise selling memberships, consulting, real estate, and just about anything else with three options. Here's a cheap lot, here's an expensive lot, here's a lot with a great view that's attractively priced.

Package in Groups of Three

Take a look at your offerings and group them into three distinctly different programs. If you have a more complicated product, with say nine options, either simplify the offerings, or use three choices to get to the second three, and three more to make the final choice. This way the prospect is always focused on smaller and easier decisions.

Too many pricing options confuse your prospects.

Confusion causes fear.
Fear causes paralysis, not action!

CHAPTER 32

How to Quickly Raise $250,000 in Cash without a Loan, a Rich Uncle, or a GUN!

All businesses struggle for money at one time or another. All need cash to expand or for "one-of" special projects. But few ever look at the diamonds under their feet as the source of their funding. Instead they go through the arduous process of applying for bank loans or tapping friends and family. There is an easier way and it works every time. With no interest, no family obligations, no banks, and you don't even need a gun!

I learned about the power of "cash up front" in the karate business but I have used it in hundreds of the businesses I have helped since. The principle is ridiculously easy, yet it's one that few people ever consider because as the numbers get bigger people often get scared. What if they turn me down? What if they ask for their money back? What if my business fails?

In the karate business, as in the health club business, the REALLY big profits come from the cash-outs, not the monthly dues! A cash-out was a student who would pay in advance for three years of lessons packaged as a "Black Belt Club Program." I tried to get one cash-out a week. Less than 5% of students ever stayed long enough to get a black belt. Most quit after four to six months but always intended to come back. So in my entire time in the business I had only one person ask for their money back — which I gave him. This works for golf lessons, dance lessons, memberships, and personal service contracts of all kinds!

I had a golf club call me and tell me they were having a bad year and were going to miss budget by $250,000. Could I help? Yes, simply sell five lifetime memberships for $60,000 and you turn a bad situation into a good one. As usual, the partner did not believe this was possible since the yearly membership was $5,000. I suggested he start with a local car dealer and sure enough he called back a few days later shocked that the first person he had asked actually said YES!

I astonished a 20-year golf teaching veteran by telling him to sell unlimited lessons for the year rather than by the hour. 20 different people paid him $5,000 and the most avid took under 20 lessons. The following year 18 renewed, they just loved the idea of having their own personal pro. This tripled the pro's income!

I have helped hundreds of teaching pros do this exact same thing! One 28-year-old assistant pro made $32,000 in a month, more than his yearly salary, by simply selling a year's worth of lessons instead of the traditional five or ten individual lessons!

If your salespeople do not have the skills or the balls to ask for big money — and many don't — another way to raise money is the careful use of factoring companies (selling your contracts to a third party at a discount). This can get you the up-front cash you need for expansion and, if spent or invested wisely, amounts to more than you would have realized over time, despite the discounted rate.

Your existing customers are the best and only bank you should ever need. They offer cash up front, no interest, and are pleased to help. But, you have to ask!

People don't care how much you know until they know how much you care!

Print Advertising
that Actually
Works

CHAPTER 33

It's Really No Fun Being a Lemming — They Fall Off Cliffs and Die!

When I first started in the karate business, all my advertising was done through the local *Shopper* or *Penny Saver* publications with the occasional ad in the local paper. Specifically, I ran print ads that looked just like every other karate school's ads. It was either a stern-looking black belt in a karate uniform staring out from the page with his hands on his hips or a man flying through the air about to kick someone in the head.

It never, not even for a moment, occurred to me that people would look at that ad with the photo of me doing a perfect side-kick at a student's face and ever think of themselves as the kickee rather than the kicker!

Little did I know that this photo was scaring prospects away!

But that was exactly what was happening!

I ran macho-man ads thinking everyone wanted to be a black belt while the reader was thinking, "Hell, if I go there I could lose all my teeth!" Since everyone else in the industry was running almost identical ads, I thought that must be how you do it!

Twenty years later, half the ads you see for martial arts schools still feature the guy flying through the air or the Asian master scowling at the camera. Similarly, golf clubs run identical ads in local papers and golf guides, hotels in hotel guides and travel magazines, manufacturers in trade rags, retailers and car dealers in the Sunday newspapers, and so on.

The next time you are tempted to run an ad that looks more or less like your competitors' or runs in the same place "everyone" in your business always runs ads, remember the lemming!

Just because everyone in your industry does the same thing does not make it right; in fact, it's almost certainly wrong!

CHAPTER 34

Cunningly Clueless Advertising

The ad on the following page is a witty take-off of a famous ad. The main benefit of the ad was to gratify my ego using my client's money so I could show everyone how clever I am! I was saved only by the fact that this ad actually ran as part of the *Garland Inquirer* magazine, a spoof publication that needed some fake ads to make it feel like a real magazine.

BUT...while "they" won't admit it,

Millions of dollars worth of ads are run daily, by ad agencies across the world, that have no real value to the client and serve only to boost the agencies' portfolios of pretty pieces and plastic award trophies.

In other words, run away from...

- Ads with puns as headlines instead of benefits

- Ads with no calls to action

- Ads with no offers

- Ads with no free stuff

- Ads with beautiful pictures and little or no copy

- Ads with no proof or testimonials

- And, most of all, agencies that try to tell you that

ABSOLUTE FUN.

*Unless you have a multimillion dollar "branding" budget,
to be effective, YOUR ads have to sell!*

impressions, image, and brand will help you make money! (It might — if you have $50 million to spend!)

Don't let your ad agency spend YOUR money to build their graphics and awards portfolio. DEMAND measurable results from every ad.

**Remember the acronym INCUIS:
It's Not Clever Unless It Sells!**

Following a formula like the one above won't win any awards but WILL make the phone ring.

CHAPTER 35

No Awards, Just Profits — How to Design a Winning Ad in 60 Seconds!

Okay, I know, your boss is not going to go with the previous sage advice and still wants you to run image ads, with a price point, your company's logo, and a worthless tag line. So at least let's make it better.

1. **Put the picture at the top of the page.** Make sure the picture stands out in some astonishing way!

2. **Put the headline underneath** the picture in nice, bold, easy-to-read type.

3. **Promise the reader a strong benefit.**

4. **Back up your promise with more benefits** in an easy-to-read typeface and a two-column format.

5. **Prove your promise** by using testimonials, surveys, and reports.

6. **Ask for action.** Tell the readers exactly what they should do.

7. **Offer something for free** to get the reader to register on your website. Then you can follow up forever!

8. **Change your tag line** or slogan at the bottom of the ad in favor of a strong unique selling proposition.

9. **Ask the question "So what?"** at the end of every sentence. If the sentence did not answer your question (from the customer's perspective), rewrite it.

10. **Add unique phone numbers** and web addresses to your ads so you can show your boss specifically what response *these* ads, in *this* publication, actually received. (This one will be far more productive than your previous efforts.)

**The closer you stick to this formula, the more effective your advertising will be.
No awards, but profitable!**

CHAPTER 36

Getting Inside Your Prospects' Heads with Your Marketing Message

My first huge marketing success was a $1,000 ad I ran in three editions of the local *Penny Saver* in Irvine, California. I was sitting in my small karate school one afternoon waiting for the world to discover me when a man in his forties walked in and said, "You know, I always wanted to try karate." About two hours later a woman in her mid-twenties walked in and said, "You know, I always wanted to try karate but my father would never let me. He wanted me to do girl stuff!" Later, around 5 pm, a mother walked in with her son and said, "He has always wanted to try karate and I have finally given in!"

Your photos should mirror your prospects.

Three totally different people, three identical comments, in just three hours.

Fortunately, the significance was not lost on me! I took the words I kept hearing from my customers and added a picture of a good looking blonde in a karate uniform flanked by two boys (in later versions we used a boy and a girl). They were actually smiling, maybe even having fun. Below their picture were the words, **"You always wanted to try karate, now is the time!"**

With a simple change in advertising strategy, I made more money in that month than I had in the previous year. The phone literally rang off the hook, all because the ad said what many of my prospects were actually thinking!

Listen to what your customers are saying about you and your products, services, or the benefits they derive from them.

Really listen.

Those words may be more effective in resonating with your prospects than those of any high-priced copywriter or ad agency, including me!

CHAPTER 37

He Never Cleaned His Room Before...

In many situations your marketing message must appeal to multiple people, personalities, and special interest groups — all at the same time! Like selling the sales department and the accounting department an office machine. Or selling a husband and a wife a vacation, car, or home!

Few companies are able to deal with this or, if they do, they fail to make the necessary adjustments to their marketing materials to connect with multiple audiences. It's a difficult task since in general an ad should be written with just ONE person, the buyer, in mind, but it can be done!

Here's an example:

A second major breakthrough in my karate schools came when I ran an ad of a 12-year-old boy sitting on his bed in a karate uniform. Around him all his toys and books were stacked neatly on a shelf. The headline screamed for parental attention:

**He Never Cleaned His Room Until I Took
Him to Martial Arts America!**

This was a very unusual ad — kids still wanted to take karate, but now the parents were buying in. The results were astonishing!

Never forget who the REAL customer is — it's the person who signs the checks, not necessarily the first one who reads your marketing materials!

Our follow-up Arm Your Child campaign was also very successful in feeding off what parents wanted to hear!

CHAPTER 38

Have Some Fun with Your Advertising Photos to Attract Attention!

The primary purpose of a photo in an ad is to attract the readers' attention. Never forget that! In 99% of cases pictures attract attention while words sell! (More on that later!)

Have some fun with your photos to make them stand out from all those other ads by people selling products and services like yours. Add something that REALLY catches your readers' attention. Then tie the story line back into your visual image!

You will be amazed how much more response you can generate with the addition of a simple element to your normal photograph! The UFO photo on the following page coincides with our out-of-this-world offer!

In other ads, I have added:

- dinosaurs to demonstrate the timeless beauty of a real estate development

- balloons to show freedom

- a 300-pound trout to show how good the fishing was in the Au Sable river.

- a paratrooper landing on a golf course to show marketing help was arriving, and

- a nearly-naked woman to grab male golfers' attention while highlighting spa treatments

Use surprising photos to bring attention to your message.

Adding a simple unusual element to your ad's main picture can produce an astonishing increase in readership!

They Say Beauty Is In The Eye Of The Beholder...
Garland, Michigan's Most Beautiful Resort!

There are lots of reasons why Garland is Michigan's most beautiful resort, and 72 holes of magnificent golf is just the beginning. Rolling meadows, lakes, streams, mature hardwoods and dramatic elevation changes are the backdrop to challenges that delight golfers of all abilities on our four magnificent courses.

Garland is also beautiful because it's the closest resort of all the Northern resorts to the metro Detroit area, so you get there faster and get home quicker. Plus you save gas — now that's beautiful!

Garland is beautiful once you get there because you can just park and play. ALL their courses start from a single pro shop. No loading, no driving, no waiting for FRED to show up so you can leave. In fact, no hassle at all!

Garland is beautiful because the accommodations are...well, beautiful. Choose from hotel, villa, condo or luxury on-course cabins. There's not a bad room in the place!

Garland is beautiful because they have great food, a steak house, cold beer, a Tiki bar and nightly entertainment that rocks!

Don't forget to try one of our spa treatments. After 36 holes on the links, it's a beautiful end to your day.

Garland is even more beautiful because if you are smart enough to book now and I know you are, you'll enjoy substantial discounts and VIP upgrades on one of our exciting golf packages.

Call Now
877-501-4758 or Visit
www.BeautifulGarland.com

Unusual photos make your ad stand out from the hundreds of others vying for attention!

CHAPTER 39

Why You MUST Grab Your Readers' Attention with Your Headline or Kiss Your Money Goodbye!

If you don't grab the readers by the throat with your headline, 95% of them won't make it past the first paragraph — or even your first sentence. Which means no matter how long or short, good or bad, or big or small your ad is, it won't work!

Without good — no — GREAT — headlines, everything that follows is a GIANT waste of time, money, effort, and trees, for it will most likely never be read!

This is so important that I want to say it again: **Your headline is the ad for your sales copy. Therefore, a great headline has one job and one job alone: Get the reader to actually read what comes next.** You must excite him, intrigue him, titillate him, shock him, question him, and project him into the future to show him the better "life" that can be his!

But Wait, My Clients Are Rich, Smart, and Sophisticated!

Perhaps the biggest mistake of all is to think that your clientele, your product, or your service is *above* such tactics. But these are not mere marketing tactics we are talking about

Give Me the Worst Performing Club in America and I'll Turn It Around in Six Months or Less, or Pay You $10,000 in Cash!

How sure am I that Legendary Marketing can help any club who listens and ACTS, succeed? Sure enough to put my entire reputation on the line, along with $10,000 of my hard earned cash!

Now I am only going to pick one applicant this time around and I want to get a couple of ground rules straight. I am a Marketing Legend, not a miracle worker so your club must meet the following simple conditions:

1. The greens have to have grass on them and course has to be in at least reasonable physical shape: no holes missing, swept away by floods or falling of a cliff due to earthquakes!

2. You have to have 18 holes or more.

3. There has to be more people than sheep, within 25 miles!

4. You have to have access to some basic funds to spend on collateral items. YOU WILL PAY NOTHING FOR MY SERVICES or any of my team's!

5. You have to have complete authority at the club (No 16- man committees) and agree to DO EVERYTHING I suggest!

6. Specific goals will be set upfront, which if I meet them, will result in a *sizable payout to me!*

7. If they are not met, I will donate all my time, my staff's time, resources, websites, sales training, manuals and data that I have provided in the attempt and will pay you $10,000 in CASH!

Now, if this offer does not make sense to you, than just tell me that you simply are not serious about wanting REAL results at your facility. To confidentially register, please visit now

WWW.TurnMyClubAround.Com

All the Best,

Andrew Wood
Marketing Legend

P.S. The winning club will be posted on our website next month:
WWW.LegendaryMarketing.com!

Ugly ad, great headline, great offer, great response!
We may be on to something here!

here; we are talking about something far more interesting and deep — human nature.

People's natural inquisitiveness and self-interest changes little with social or economic status. Sure the things they buy may change, but the way you attract their interest changes very little. Delude yourself that your high-end product is different and that your customers are so sophisticated that they will take your abstract headlines and write their own sales pitches in their heads…but THEY WON'T!

Your headline is the ad for your ad, make it Cunningly Clever!

CHAPTER 40

The 12 Formulas for Writing Headlines that Make Prospects Want to Read Your Copy!

There are 12 proven formulas for writing captivating headlines. Formulas!? But isn't great marketing all about creativity?

NO. Let me repeat that, NO!

Sure, creativity helps. But very often, in an effort to be creative, people ignore the basics of human nature. The end result of their efforts is a campaign that is called cute, funny, or creative, and might even win an award, but the ad BOMBS where it counts, in actually increasing YOUR RESPONSE!

Great movies are the result of great scripts, very often formulaic scripts. So, too, are most bestselling books and great sales letters, letters which ALL start with great headlines.

You can borrow winning headlines from other industries and adapt them to your needs. Some of the world's best headlines still pull responses 50 years or more after their creation. They can do this because while the world changes quickly, people do not. People today have the same basic vanities, desires, motivations, fears, and hopes as their parents and their parents' parents, albeit with more money to satisfy them!

In writing headlines, never forget that people are emotional, irrational beings who respond to *their* wants and needs, not yours!

The 12 Proven Ways to Write Cunningly Clever Headlines

1. **The Benefit Headline** — Be Slim: Lose 20 lbs in Two Weeks

2. **The Offer Headline** — Buy Now, Get One Free

3. **The Discount Headline** — Save 40%

4. **The News-Style Headline** — New Homes Selling Fast!

5. **The Bonus Headline** — Free Shipping

6. **The Testimonial Headline** — This Product Works, I Love It!

7. **The How-To Headline** — How to Get a Date Tonight

8. **The Secrets Headline** — 7 Secrets to Growing Flowers

9. **The Guarantee Headline** — Money Back If Not Happy!

10. **The Question Headline** — What Happens If You Die?

11. **The Shocking Headline** — Man Makes Millions in Bed!

12. **Headlines with Free in Them!** — Free Beer Until 8 pm!

Just like movie scripts, books, and comedians' gags, certain formulas for headlines have been proven to work. Use them!

CHAPTER 41

The Most Powerful Word in the World

The most powerful word in print ads was, is, and probably always will be: FREE!

It works in headlines, it works in copy, it works in testimonials, and it works in offers and calls to action.

- Free Trial
- Free Booklet
- Free White Paper
- Free Estimates
- Free Consultation
- Free CD
- Free Seminar
- Free DVD
- Free Check Up

- Free Analysis
- Free Bonus
- Free Gift
- Free Guide
- Free Rooms
- Free Internet
- Free Breakfast
- Free Car Wash
- Free Maps

Sometimes it's the most basic of changes that produce the most astonishing results. Like when I talked a daily-fee golf course into advertising FREE golf for a month during their slow, early-spring season. They built a database of 9,857 prospects in

Win a FREE Weekend Golf Package for
You and Seven Guests Valued at Over $3,000

Register **NOW** to win this amazing package at **www.SycuanResortFreeStay.com** and you will be immediately entered into our drawing to receive four deluxe guest rooms, two days unlimited golf including golf cart and a complimentary dinner with dessert for everyone... and automatically become eligible to receive future specials and promotions as well.

Sycuan Resort offers all the amenities of a first class destination resort with a 103 room lodge and 54 holes of spectacular golf. This package is valued at over $3,000.

www.SycuanResortFreeStay.com
CALL NOW! 1-888-556-2058

*A simple but great example of an effective ad for building
a database of prospects!*

30 days! Then, armed with all those golfers' emails, they went on to dominate their market!

FREE removes risks and adds value while increasing readership and response. What can you do with this most magical of words to increase your results?

Use "FREE" with a liberal sprinkling of the word "YOU" whenever you can in print ads. Beware: This doesn't work in emails as FREE often triggers the spam filter.

CHAPTER 42

How to Get a Thousand Times More Value from Your Print Ads — Stop Trying to Sell

Most print advertising is a gigantic waste of time, money, and trees! But fortunately there is a solution and a way to maximize your return on print ads.

- Stop advertising to build your brand.

- Stop advertising to keep "top of the mind" awareness.

- Stop advertising to build your image.

- Stop advertising to feed your owner's ego.

- Stop advertising price points or specials.

- Stop running coupons (unless redeemed on your website).

- Stop advertising new products or services.

- Stop advertising because all your competition does.

Instead:

- Start advertising.

- Keep advertising.

- And ONLY advertise to build your database of quality leads.

Make every ad a reason to register on your website or call a toll-free number. Get prospects to put their hands up and say, "YES, I am interested in your product or service," by giving you their names, phone numbers, and emails, and whatever data you need to segment your leads into groups for future sales.

Use your print ads solely to create leads by driving people to your website or getting them to call your 800 number. You will find it an astonishingly more effective strategy than whatever you are doing now!

Plus, once you have their info, or at least their email address, you can follow up forever almost free!

CHAPTER 43

How to Cut Your Ad Budget in Half with No Loss of Response!

Since my karate school was positioned near the border of multiple zones, I ran ads in all five editions of my local *Penny Saver* for over a year. Then, one rainy afternoon, for no particular reason, I started putting pins in the oversized street map of the city I had hanging in my back office just to see where my students were actually coming from.

Next I traced the *Penny Saver* zones in red marker. I was astonished to find that 95% of my students came from just *two zones*, with just a handful more from the closest and most affluent zone to my school.

I later found out that people don't like crossing bridges, freeways, rivers, railway lines, busy intersections, and city, county, or state boundaries. In fact, faced with any of these obstacles, people will often drive several miles in the other direction. But I digress…

Armed with this astonishing information of where my customers actually came from, I told my rep to run ads in only two of the five zones, cutting my ad budget by 60%. Later I reduced it again by an additional 40% when I ran half-page ads instead of full-page ads. Neither of these moves, which saved me a whopping 70% of my ad budget, reduced my response by one iota!

It was primitive tracking but it was enough to focus my attention on tracking results from every campaign since it's something few people ever do!

It was this experience that ultimately lead me to develop the ad tracking tool in Marketing Commander (a tool so sophisticated that it tracks everything, even phone calls to a specific campaign).

Do you know exactly where your customers come from? If not, find out. Then advertise only in those states, counties, regions, cities, postal codes, developments, or streets!

5

Turning Your Website into a Money-Making Marketing Machine

CHAPTER 44

How I Turned 360,000 Website Visitors into Dust Instead of Cash!

I was lucky to get involved in web activities early. I built my first site in 1994 — the dinosaur era in web terms. It was an eight-page electronic brochure for Martial Arts America that cost me $10,000. I had no clue what I was doing or what the Internet would become, I just thought it was cool!

The site was getting huge traffic — 30,000 visitors a month — not because we were doing anything to promote it but because there really weren't that many sites to visit!

I took NO advantage whatsoever of this traffic. I didn't capture visitors' names, I had no booking engine, and I didn't have a shopping cart. Nor did I change the content to get people to come back. Therefore I provided one-time information to hundreds of thousands of people without making a dime in actual cash or finding out who these people really were!

Sadly, even today, this is how the majority of websites still operate because business owners, CEOs, and even marketing managers don't understand what the true purpose of their websites should be!

Your website should be the absolute foundation of all your marketing activities, the command-and-control center of everything you do in the name of marketing. Every campaign whether online or offline should be built around your website and be aimed at driving prospects and customers to your website to **capture their interest** in a product or service you offer and report in detail on how they got there!

Think about your website:

- It is the only employee you have who never calls in sick. It books business, sells products, and answers questions 24 hours a day.

- It's the only marketing you have that can send instant and personalized responses to prospective customers at 3 am on a Sunday morning by using pre-programmed autoresponders and follow-up letters.

- It's the only marketing you have that can collect detailed information on prospects while you sleep by using dynamic request forms.

- It's the only marketing you can do that incrementally lowers your future marketing costs with almost every visit to your website.

There is no **more important marketing tool at your business than your website.** Yet most businesses, even large ones, are content to trade style for substance rather than make the commitment to building worldclass websites with back-end tools that increase business faster than the national debt.

Even where businesses have made substantial investments with ad agencies or web design companies, they almost always miss the mark. **While these vendors understand the technology and design aspects, they DO NOT understand the marketing aspects** of a truly great website.

Anyone over 12 years old can design a good-looking website in about 4 hours! And don't let anyone fool you, any decent web team can duplicate the look and feel of any website in the world you happen to like, in about 8 hours.

Design is the easy part of the web business, the part anyone can do! (However, a great many designs are counterproductive to using your site to get response.) It's the capability to collect data on the front end and the functionality to respond and report on the back end that REALLY count!

Your website cannot just be pretty, it has to be a marketing machine with a sophisticated back end to be an effective tool; 98% are not!

Make your website the foundation of your entire marketing plan. Everything from capturing leads to reporting on ads should revolve around your website!

CHAPTER 45

Why Your Current Website Isn't Making You Any Money!

Almost certainly your website is not nearly as good as it should be and it doesn't matter how much you spent on it — $100,000 websites are likely to be just as poor at generating business as $500 websites. As astonishing as this may sound, I have seen it time and time again.

Just this week we began working with a new partner, a large hotel that spent over $100,000 last year on a flash-based website "masterpiece" that scored a whopping three out of ten on our marketing effectiveness test! Our new partners routinely dump websites that they spent five or ten times the money on for 90% less functionality than provided by our Marketing Commander solution.

But you be the judge of your site…

Take This Quick Test to Find Out How Effective Your Website Is Where It Matters

Yes No

1. Do you have at least five different ways to collect prospect data (LEADS) on your site? He with the *biggest and best* database wins!   ☐   ☐

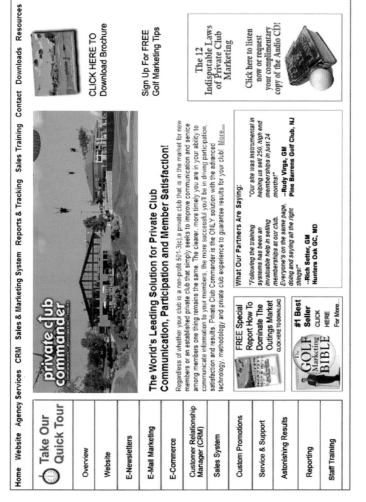

Clean, functional, easy to navigate, nice flash show, testimonials and FIVE different ways to collect prospect data!

Yes   No

2. Does your website respond AUTOMATICALLY to requests with personalized emails based **on your visitors' answers to questions about their preferences.** (That way you ONLY send your visitors those offers to which they are most likely to respond.) ☐ ☐

3. Can you make changes to your site or do an email blast yourself if you happen to have a brilliant idea at 2 am — without calling anyone and without any computer experience necessary? Speed is a strategy! ☐ ☐

4. Can you preprogram your marketing calendar into your site so it automatically contacts your customers with timely updates on everything your business offers, driving up incremental revenue in every area? ☐ ☐

5. Can your site send A/B email offers to a small sampling of your database to see which works best and then automatically send the winning offer to everyone? ☐ ☐

6. Does each and every page of your site have great headlines, compelling copy, a complete sales pitch, testimonials, and a call for action? ☐ ☐

7. Can your prospects make DETAILED requests at your site and can you preprogram your site with customized sales letters to automatically follow up to all requests, based on the prospects' specific interests? ☐ ☐

Yes　No

8. Does your site update itself with new content automatically each month so there are always fresh articles — how-to items, ideas, and humor to read, appropriately customized for our customers? Are you the KING of content in your industry?　☐　☐

9. Does your website automatically send you detailed campaign reports every week showing the exact response of every campaign, including how many people visited your site, downloaded your literature, entered their data, made requests, and called your campaign-specific phone number?　☐　☐

10. Does your website provide a report that gives you an exact cost per lead on every dollar spent in the name of marketing?　☐　☐

To see a detailed sample report, go to:

www.CunninglyCleverMarketing.com

If you answered no to more than four of these questions, you do not have a marketing machine — you have a typically average website — one that's little more than an electronic billboard. It looks pretty, but does little to help you increase your business!

CHAPTER 46

Why Your Company's Current Web Strategy Is Almost Certainly Wrong — and Costing You Millions in Lost Revenue!

Ask a number of people what the most important function of their company's website is and you are liable to hear a good many answers about providing information, selling goods, and increasing business. Rarely, if ever, will you hear the answer that I consider paramount to online success.

The number one purpose of a website should be to generate qualified leads. If you focus all your efforts on that, everything else will fall into place. But if you focus only on selling, you may run out of prospects!

Every single bit of marketing you do should focus on driving people to your website to register and answer questions about their habits, wants, and needs.

All ads, sales letters, brochures, promotions, TV, radio, and e-blasts should drive people to your website to register!

If you fail to capture visitors' data, you won't know who they are and you cannot follow up with them at little or no cost in the future.

This is a great website with lots of testimonials, a real sales pitch for the service, upcoming promotions at the top and, not one, but four ways to capture data on the home page alone!!

Once registered, your website can follow up with an unlimited number of offers customized to that person's unique profile. You can, of course, also use this valuable data for phone sales and direct mail — but ONLY if you collect it!

Change your entire marketing strategy to make building a huge database of qualified prospects through your website your number one goal. If you do this, sales will surely follow!

CHAPTER 47

Rapidly Building Your Prospect Database

Do you buy lotto tickets or enter contests? Lots of people do although I rarely do myself. How about discounts — will you register on a website to get one? Perhaps you would not respond to any of these methods — but what if you got an incentive like a free hotel room or a cabin upgrade?

The fact of the matter is, different people respond to different options. I personally like getting information on products and services I happen to be interested in. For this I will gladly part with my information. Other people have little interest in downloading brochures or white papers but will register to watch a video or online demo. Still others will opt for VIP clubs, discounts, or loyalty-type programs.

Basically, you can group people into six categories:

- contest people

- club people

- discount people

- incentive people

- information people, and

- crossovers (those who respond to multiple types of offers)

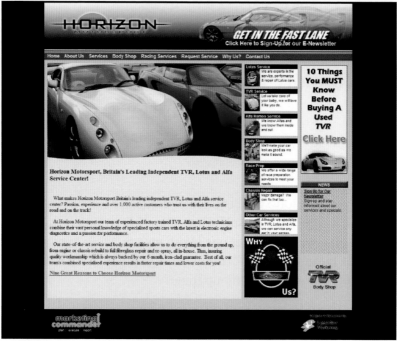

This site uses three different ways to collect data on the home page.

Building Your Database

The six most successful techniques for building a database are:

1. Make customers and prospects register online for any special offer or coupon to be validated. For example, at one of our automobile partners we offered a 15% discount on their next service if customers would register online and answer a few questions about their wants, needs, and preferences. This, of course, provided a great deal of useful data. The company also offered a free newsletter and a model-specific guide to buying a used car.

2. Run monthly promos with great prizes and publicize that someone actually won! Win a Free Vacation at _____, Win a Free Shopping Spree, Win a $500 gift certificate, and so on.

Register on this site to win a month's FREE rent!

3. Offer something of value free in return for information. With our golf course clients, we offer a free round of golf. With hotels, we offer a free room night (with both of these types of businesses we do it at off-peak times only). At Legendary Marketing, we offer a free marketing evaluation.

There is a lot going on at this site but there's a lot going on at the resort. Everything you could want is easy to find right on the home page! This site collected over 58,000 prospect names in the last three years!!

4. Use online booking engines, surveys, and shopping carts to collect data. This is a really painless way to get data.

5. Ask customers at the counter to fill in a card and provide a spiff for doing so — free coffee, free lunch, free souvenir booklet, and so forth.

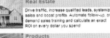

*My company has designed over 1,000 different websites. Clients want this,
clients want that — but it pays to remember that only a
handful of designs produce optimum marketing results!*

6. Last, and very often one of the best, use FREE downloads of information: booklets, stories, tips, jokes, etc. At the Auto Toy Store we offer a free booklet on what to look for and what to avoid in buying a used Ferrari. At Frost Wines we offer a golf-tips booklet written by the vineyard owner and PGA Tour star David Frost. At MarketingCommander.com and

LegendaryMarketing.com we offer various booklets, white papers, and special reports, all of which help us generate a substantial number of leads.

Since different people respond to different methods, you must use ALL methods at your disposal to collect data from your website. That means employing five different ways of collecting information, not the one or two you find on most websites!

CHAPTER 48

The Unknown and Largely Ignored Secrets of Effective Website Design

Most people know what they like, BUT — and it's a big BUT—they rarely know what works when it comes to web design. Here are some key secrets to getting the most from your site's design.

Always choose substance, functionality, and ease of use over style! This does not mean your site cannot be stylish, but do not let style destroy functionality and effectiveness.

Forget intro pages where you make people wait for a Flash show before they get into your site. Those pages are annoying and a great way to get a visitor to hit the back button.

Make sure your site loads fast!

Put the main menu at the top or on the left, never at the right or at the bottom. Depending on users' screen sizes, the menu may disappear from view.

Make your flash-show large enough to be impressive and showcase your business in pictures.

Design your home page in such a way that keeps all of your upcoming events, products, and offers right in front of your visitors. This can either be a banner ad that changes itself with each new offer or scrolling news if more appropriate for

This website is clean, easy to navigate, and easy to read. It's easy to find what you want. Rotating offers collect data.

your industry. Don't make visitors log in and go look for this information!

You can also use hover pages for this but don't overuse them. Change the featured product often.

If you want new customers, make sure you **have a prominent box on your home page that collects data** and offers a quick and prominent route to more information about your products and services.

Have enough copy on your home page to provide a decent overview of your business and help aid your placement in search engine rankings. This means, normally at least 150–200 words minimum; 400 words are better. Most web designers act as if they are afraid of words or feel that words pollute their beautiful designs. IGNORE them; you need text to sell your visitor and to help generate good search engine rankings. Always err on the side of too much information and you will hardly ever go wrong. People will decide for themselves what information is relevant to them and what is too much! (Much more on this later.)

Make your copy large enough to read, in a simple typeface with little or no background color. Over 60% of all websites are unreadable because they are created by teenagers with great eyesight. Anything less than 10-point Times is unacceptable and bigger is always better. Not from a design viewpoint, but from a RESULTS viewpoint!

The same holds true for reverse type or any graphical element that makes reading your site harder; JUST **DON'T** DO IT!

Make sure all your key pages have complete sales presentations, not just bullet points. Not having sales presentations is an elementary Marketing-101 error made by 99% of all websites!

Make the log in for members, guests, customers, or partners easy to find.

Make sure the visitor's "eye path" is simple and straightforward. People read from top to bottom and left to right. Too many distractions cause a pinball effect — that never helps results.

Put a call to action at the bottom of every page.

Put testimonials at the top of every page.

Make all icons, or thumbnails clickable. Don't make visitors work to find the word to click on; make it easy.

*Easy to navigate, easy to read, graphically pleasing, and
collects data — good site!*

Your graphic designer, web company, and ad agency won't like
following these principles, but your accountant will when he sees
how much more effective your site is at generating business!

**The closer you stick to these design guidelines,
the more effective your website will be.**

CHAPTER 49

How Much Information Is Too Much Information on Your Website?

THE ANSWER MAY SHOCK YOU! Do you know what the number one complaint of web surfers is? Drum roll...not enough information once they get to a site.

There are few things more frustrating than surfing around the web for an hour only to find that the site you thought was perfect says call for more info and it's 10:23 pm!

It's very difficult to get people to understand this important concept since very few of the people reading this book at this very moment will be in the market for, say, a 10-acre horse a farm in Hernando, Florida. Therefore most of you are not likely to be all that interested in reading about the new eight-stall barn, the fencing, the duck pond, and the mature oak trees dripping with Spanish moss. Since you have no immediate need or desire for this product, you will have no particular interest in what follows. Whether the information came in the mail or you stumbled across it on a website, you would not even give it a second glance, let alone read the whole thing.

Who would read a four-page sales pitch on this farm? NO ONE! No one, that is, who is not really interested in buying a horse farm in Florida — and that, my friends, is the POINT!

You SHOULD ALWAYS write copy for the small percentage

of people who actually want to BUY what YOU have to SELL!

People who buy anything, from sunscreen to a home, car, a flat screen, or cosmetic dental work, want to know what they are getting for their money. They want details; they want reasons to buy; they want proof to back up the emotional response they had to your headline. They want enough information to justify taking the next step!

Heck, you have read page after page in this book, because you are INTERESTED in marketing success. I rest my case!

There are hundreds of people who will disagree with the above statement, but NONE of them will have PROOF or actually make their living selling and marketing anything of value!

The more you tell, the more you sell!!!

Repeat this to yourself until it's etched in your brain like that annoying tune from "It's a Small World!"

CHAPTER 50

The Importance of Being Content Rich If You Don't Want to Be Poor!

Being a content-rich website is critically important if you want to attract, retain, and keep visitors coming back. This is one of the key areas where small entrepreneurs can run circles around their large corporate competition and where you really can level the playing field.

Your site needs articles, reviews, videos, audios, photos, testimonials, surveys, special reports, resources, links, top-ten lists, jokes, cartoons, forums, Q&As, blogs, and anything else that makes sense in your industry to provide additional value to your customers and prospects!

Because...

The more information you have on your products, services, uses, and partnerships, the more likely a visitor will find something of interest.

The more interesting your how-to articles, experience articles, reviews, and lists, and the more useful your content is to other sites, the more likely they are to link to your sites as a resource. This brings you extra traffic at no cost!

The more relevant the content you have on your site, the more likely people are to stay longer. The longer they stay, the more likely they are to buy or at least refer your site.

The more relevant the content you have on your site, the more useful it will be in helping you gain top search engine rankings.

The more relevant the content you have on your site, the more credible your company is as an expert and solution.

My good friend Marcus Addolfson was my first employee at Legendary Marketing. While in high school he designed a site for users of the Visor product. Over the years he built a loyal following for all of the content, forums, and product reviews he posted. It bumbled along for a few years until the smart-phone revolution exploded. When it did his site, www.SmartPhonePros.com became the center of attention. He went from making a few thousands dollars a month to earning over a million a month and being one of the fastest growing companies in the country. While he sells phone accessories you could buy anywhere, his content made him the choice of thousands of customers who trusted his reviews and expertise.

Most websites are woefully short of great content. To see examples with good content, visit:

www.CunninglyCleverMarketing.com

Content is king; it's good to be king!

CHAPTER 51

Why Your Website Should Be an Ad Salesman's Worst Nightmare!

One tool a great website should have is the ability to plan, execute, and track all of your various marketing campaigns. This includes both internal and external marketing, both on and off the web. This allows you to see and track exactly how many phone calls, web visits, and requests you got from each print ad, e-blast, or direct-mail campaign.

It's currently 7:52 am — do you know if your marketing is REALLY working?

For years now, I have been preaching the value of tracking all of your marketing. **After all, if you don't track each campaign, how do you know whether it is working?** Most people simply don't track their results other than the occasional coupon count. Instead, they judge their marketing's success or failure on what comes in at the till. Gross revenues are a measurement as variable in any given week, as, say, the weather!

Even those clients that took my advice and have 20 plus website addresses and multiple 800 numbers to track each campaign don't actually look at their results. Why? Because they rarely go to the enormous trouble of breaking out 20 phone bills, matching the numbers to a specific ad or mailing list, and then tabulating all the results in an Excel spreadsheet. It's boring, painstaking work that not surprisingly no one ever seems to find the time to do.

Which is why I am so excited about our new membership campaign for a partner in Westchester, New York. This particular campaign has been set up in Marketing Commander so that every phone call, every web visit, and every contact point reports in real time right on their website.

For this campaign we have rented seven different mailing lists. Each list has its own website address and its own 800 number, all of which forward to the partner after one ring on our server. As soon as the first mailing hits, the manager will be able to view the exact number of calls and visits that each list generates.

When we are done we will all be able to CLEARLY see which lists produced the most leads, which lists were the most effective at producing sales, and which lists didn't work at all. **It will also give us an accurate count on how many leads came in by phone, rather than relying on a receptionist to keep count with pen and paper.** This, of course, is invaluable in actually determining the closing ratio between leads and conversion to sales.

This is critical information, available in real time so that future campaigns can be tweaked in the right direction. Our partners will know the exact cost of every lead, not just on this direct-mail campaign but on every print ad, every e-blast — in fact, on every promotion ever done in the name of marketing.

This, of course, allows them to direct money only at the ad-media that produce the greatest response. It allows them to track A/B offers and see which offer pulls the most business. It allows them to do small test runs before they roll out a large campaign, and in makes their marketing more effective on a daily, or even hourly basis in the case of a large email blast.

Marketing Commander is the only product in the world that allows you to do this. The amount of marketing money that this tracking feature alone could save you and, in fact, make you, over the next couple of years, is staggering.

Imagine the face of the media rep next time he comes calling and you print out a report showing exactly how many phone calls and web visits you got from his ad along with an exact cost per lead. ...Makes you smile just thinking about it, doesn't it?

How many inquiries did you get last year? If you have the right website technology, you could pull up the data in the next five seconds! (More on this critical topic in the section on Marketing Sabotage.)

Your website technology should be capable of tracking and reporting on all of your marketing campaigns, including your off-line campaigns and inbound calls!

CHAPTER 52

The Great Search Engine Con —
Are You a Victim?

Everywhere you look (including some of my old work), you're told search engine positioning is 95% of all web traffic. It is — IF you're renting villas in Italy, selling super luxury cars, or if you have a hotel located in a strong destination market like Orlando, Napa Valley, or perhaps Palm Springs. BUT before you go to the trouble and expense of a search engine optimization program, consider these facts:

- Our highest-traffic resort website got over 300,000 unique visitors last year and is generally found under its key term on page one in a Google search. Yet ONLY 15 percent of their traffic was generated from the search engines. Seventeen percent was generated from links with other sites and the remaining 236,000 visits were generated from their proprietary database of 78,000 guests!!!

- The Legendary Marketing site has ranked in one of the top three positions in Google for well over five years. And yet Google has generated only 164 visitors so far this year. This is a TINY percentage of our traffic, which is well over 20,000 visitors a month!

Once again, the key to the high number of visits is not a high search-engine ranking, but a database of 25,000 people who subscribe to our weekly newsletter.

Am I saying that search-engine positioning is not important? HECK NO! But before you spend a great deal of time, money, and effort to improve your site's rankings, look at how much traffic any given search terms generates.

For example, different variations of "ORLANDO" and "GOLF" bring up 3,000–5,000 searches a day in-season, which is obviously well worth a shot at getting. You will, of course, be competing with every major hotel chain in the world, every major tour operator, and a local outfit called Disney, but, hey, no one said it would be easy!

On the flip side of the scale, you'd be shocked at how little traffic a term like "MN Golf Resorts" might generate; recently it was *fewer than 50 searches a day* and that counts golf schools <u>and</u> a bunch of other Minnesota golf-related terms.

For businesses drawing their business from a 30-mile radius and not in a major metropolis or destination area, the effort at achieving search-engine prominence is very often not worth the money, which can range from a few hundred dollars a month to a few thousand!

5 Ways to Get Better Search-Engine Positioning

1. Do you own URLs that include your key words or phrases like, "Orlando Hotel Finder," or "Atlanta Cigar Company." This is an easy way to boost rankings.

2. Look at the copy on your home page. Does it repeat the key word or phrase you want to achieve ranking for? The more copy you have that includes key words, the more chance you have of good rankings. (NOTE:

Very often high ranking sites have copy that reads poorly but helps ranking; that's the trade off!)

3. Do you have at least 50 inbound links (400 links is better!) from other sites that mention your key word or phrase in the link? For example, if you're selling golf homes in Vail, you would ensure that your inbound links said "Vail Ski Homes," rather than the actual name of your property. This is because search engines rank the words in the link.

4. Buy your position. This is a tricky business as very often words are bid up far beyond their true value. But it can be an excellent way to test the market without spending much money. If it works, keep doing it!

5. Hire someone to provide an optimization plan. We even offer this service but — I warn you — I talk more people *out* of doing this than I talk into it! It has to make sense before I'll take your money!

A final warning: Many of my partners get weekly solicitations from outfits telling them that there are all kinds of problems with their site that hurt their search engine rankings. Most of these are automatically generated emails from dubious software that reports on such things. I called a couple of these companies and questioned their findings.

"Are you sure if I do these three things you suggest that I will get higher rankings?"

"Yes," they say.

"And," I continue, "would it be correct to say that with all the problems with current site's set up, I have no way of ever getting a decent ranking?"

"Yes, I'm afraid that it would be very difficult to get your current site ranked high " (because of this or that).

"Really," I said. "This site has been ranked number one in Google for seven years and three months, how much higher do you think I can get if I pay you $500 a month?

The silence was deafening!

Even when companies can get you higher rankings, don't confuse traffic with income. It's very easy to double or triple site visits and not sell a dime more in product if the visitors are not the right type of visitors!

Search engine tactics change all the time. See the marketing vault for the very latest information.

Search engines are important, BUT building your own database of prospects is far more important!

Don't get conned!

6

*Cunningly Clever
Email*

CHAPTER 53

Content Is King When It Comes to Building Lists, Traffic, and Income!

In 1998 I was looking to get out of the martial arts business and do something else, but I wanted to keep the income coming in while I figured out what to do next.

The answer was MartialArtsBusiness.com. I built a nice but simple site. We began populating it with relevant content and set out to build an email list. I spent several weeks tracking down every website I could find that was involved in martial arts. Once there, I copied down their contact emails. At the same time I begged or bought the few lists that vendors had of school owners, and I eventually came up with just over 10,000 emails.

I emailed the people on the list a free content-rich newsletter and kept sending it every week. Now, in the purest sense, I was sending them spam. I had not asked their permission to be opted in. Back then, though, spam was far less of a problem than it is today and I had very few complaints or requests to "un-subscribe." **I was sending a relevant newsletter to a very specific business group.** Within a few weeks the site, which was a monthly subscription-based model, was doing $10,000 a month (and eventually got over $20,000)!

Content rich e-newsletters drive business no matter what your business!

A short time later I decided to start my golf marketing business and did the exact same thing. I visited every golf course I could find online, harvested their emails, and began sending them my newsletter. While the number of people who opted out was larger than in the karate business, it was still an insignificant number, especially compared to the number of people who were willingly opting in when people passed the newsletters around. Again, technically spam, but with an easy and visible unsubscribe, I had very few problems. The newsletter grew my business rapidly!

These days it's far more difficult to do this, although you are, under the CanAM spam act, allowed to send one solicitation to ask someone to receive your emails. In a business-to-business situation, this still can work to jump-start your online efforts although you have to be very careful. It takes VERY FEW complaints to your ISP (Internet service provider) to get your site shut down!

That's why it's best to use all of your off-line marketing to drive people to your site and build your opt-in list quickly!

That's also why you need a great e-newsletter full of relevant content so people will read it, opt in, and pass it on to others!

Include articles on how to use your products or services to better your readers' lives. Back it up with histories of other customers who have succeeded with your ideas. Include articles that demonstrate your superior expertise and knowledge of your industry. And most of all, use unique and personalized stories that they can't get anywhere else! Put your company's personality into your newsletter so it stands out from others!

You can't just send out promos for your products and services; you must engage, entertain, interact with, and connect with your readers!

GARLAND
R E S O R T

CLICK HERE
FOR
*Holiday
events*

CLICK HERE &
Make A
RESERVATION

20 Reasons
to Book
Your Next
MeetingAt
Garland

WINTER ISSUE::

*"Garland is like Planet Snow-
mobile, it's got everything you
need for a wonderful time in
one convenient place!"*
- Sandy Sharp, Flint

**If you love winter time sports, here is what
we have to offer:**

**Garland USA is Michigan's No.1 resort for
snowmobiling**

When you make Garland your snowmobile headquarters you'll be
connected to hundreds of miles of groomed state and county wilderness trails, ranked among the finest in Michigan. Bring your own
machine or rent one of the top quality models. **continue**
hours of spectacular winter fun! We will teach you how to use our
snowmobiles. And there is secure, lit parking for all trailers and
machines.

*"Ski, eat, ski eat, ski, eat is that
all there is? ... Don't change a
thing we love it!"*
- Joe & Peggy Larson,
Port Huron

**Rejuvenate your body and your mind with
cross-country skiing at Garland**

*"Ski, eat, ski eat, ski, eat is that all there is
Don't change a thing we love it!"*
- Joe & Peggy Larson,
Port Huron

Cross country skiing at Garland will take you through our majestic
snow covered pines, streams and forests for an unforgettable adven-
ture. Here on our hundreds of miles of pristine trails you will exercise
your body and rejuvenate your mind. Enjoy stress free living as you
breathe our crystal-clear air and commune with nature, safe in the
knowledge that your cell phone won't work, even if you **continue**

*"Garland is like Planet Snow-
mobile, it's got everything you
need for a wonderful time in
one convenient place!"*
- Sandy Sharp, Flint

**Ride in a horse-drawn sleigh for the ultimate
get-away-from-it-all experience**

What would winter be without a horse drawn sleigh ride? That would
be like playing golf in Michigan without playing at Garland! It just
wouldn't be right! We feature 16-person sleighs in operation every
weekend during the winter. One of the highlights of the **continue**

CALL NOW 1-877-4GARLAND OR CLICK HERE FOR RESERVATIONS

An effective ezine combines content with timely promotions !

For samples of content-rich ezines go to:

www.CunninglyCleverMarketing.com

**Content-rich newsletters are the key to building
your online business.**

CHAPTER 54

The Changing Face of Email Marketing — How to Boost Your Delivery Rates!

Email marketing is getting tougher, much tougher. Less and less email is reaching its intended recipients. ISPs are blocking more and more email; spam filters and firewalls are blocking more email; and end users themselves are doing the rest by simply not opening what does get through. Delivery and open rates are at their lowest point ever. So what's a business to do to get email open rates up?

1. **Make re-opting in a strong and never-ending part of your online marketing.** Contests, pdf downloads, and special offers are not there just to grow your list, they are also there to maintain it. We now offer our partners new promotions every month or so to help with this process. From complimentary vacations at top golf resorts to exclusive content, we are always looking for new ways to get customers to re-opt in and update their data. YOU MUST DO THE SAME at least quarterly to keep your data fresh.

2. **Send only those offers that are of interest to that person.** Don't send offers for fishing vacations to people who don't fish or wine tasting to people who don't drink. If you have the right back-end, like Marketing Commander, it will sort your contact

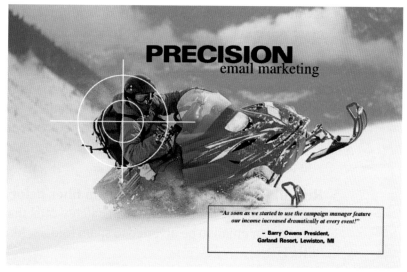

For an astoninshingly better response, send specific offers only to those people who have indicated their interest.

point data automatically to send email offers only to those people most likely to respond based on their answers to your questions. **This increases response rates dramatically and decreases opt-outs.**

With our resort partners, we set up email blasts based on the activities the guests have told us they enjoy through web surveys and contests. If you said snow-mobiling was something you enjoy, come November, you'd receive the first of five preprogrammed campaigns.

3. **Set up a dedicated email server,** not one that is shared with anyone else. That way you won't get blocked for their mistakes. ISPs block IP numbers, not individual businesses. If someone using your email service is spamming, you all get blocked!

4. **Remove all bounced and bad emails at once.** The more you bounce bad emails, the more likely you are to be blocked. Very few companies spend any time maintaining their lists so 60% of the emails they have are bad to begin with. Therefore, they are getting false reports. Get your list clean so you can really see what your open rates are! They may be better than you think, it's just that your list may be worse than you think!

5. **Run all your emails through a spam filter before you send them.** That way you can catch words that trigger your email to be diverted to spam folders, like "FREE"!

6. **Ask your readers to put you on their personal safe lists.**

7. **Make sure your website provider is white listed** with all the top ISPs. We are, but it still does not stop you from getting blocked, it only helps.

8. **Never import unknown lists into your database.** Now more than ever your lists have to be opt in! If you are going to use lists you have acquired, use a different list server than the one you usually do!

9. **Use direct mail at least four times a year** to reach your database with an offer that encourages them to re-sign up on your website, giving you their latest email and information. Snail mail addresses stay current far longer than emails (and they'll forward better). Many people are very frustrated with the fact that a large percentage of their emails are no good, but they overlook the fact that a huge percentage of the postal addresses they have collected from their

website *are* good. DO NOT miss the opportunity to use direct mail. The mailing lists you have collected from your website will produce SUPERIOR results to any other form of marketing if you send them the right offer.

10. **Pay careful attention to your subject line:** The success of your email will live and die on it!

Subscribe to these ten commandments of email marketing to boost your response rates.

CHAPTER 55

20 Quick Ways to Get Opt-In Subscribers for Your Ezine and Offers!

One of the most powerful ways to increase your web traffic and build your brand is, of course, to publish your own electronic newsletter, commonly called an ezine. This allows you to demonstrate your expertise and showcase your products or specials. It gives you instant access to hundreds or even thousands of people at virtually no cost! The question is how do you get visitors to your site to sign up for your ezine.

1. **Bribe them!** At one site we offered a FREE $20 gift certificate for signing up. This was done automatically by sending the subscriber an email with a promo code as soon as they signed up.

2. **Run a contest with a valuable prize.** At most of our golf course partners' sites, you can enter a contest to win a free year of membership worth $5,000 and up when you sign up.

3. **Offer a free chapter.** At a number of book sites you can get the first chapter of the e-book, free of charge, if you sign up.

4. Let your visitors know that a subscription to your ezine is free **for a limited time only!**

5. **Offer your visitors free software if they subscribe.** Many sites do this and since the software can be downloaded there is no out-of-pocket cost.

6. **Offer visitors access to a private members-only** part of your website if they subscribe. At MartialArtsBusiness.com we had three levels of access: 1) general, to get people interested; 2) sign up, which was free and got you a little more access; or 3) paid, with full access.

7. Many ezines **offer new subscribers a free advertisement** for their own products or services in the ezine if they subscribe.

8. **Offer your visitors a free tangible gift** (like a coffee mug or a T-shirt) if they subscribe!

9. Tell your visitors that **they have the right to republish your articles** in their own ezines if they subscribe to yours!

10. You can tease visitors by letting them know that **special hot deals can only be had** by being on your email list!

11. You could offer your visitors a free service if they subscribe, such as a **FREE 15-minute consultation.**

12. **Let your visitors know what the value** of your ezine is by placing a dollar amount on it — for example, "This information is worth $197, but is yours free if you sign up now!"

13. Tell your visitors that you **offer original content** not found in any other place.

14. **Respond to others' forum posts,** mentioning your ezine as an answer to their specific questions.

15. Include a direct message **inviting existing subscribers to pass along your ezine** to someone else at the bottom of every publication. You'll be amazed how many extra subscribers you can generate just by making this suggestion.

16. **Publish testimonials about your ezine** throughout your website so people hear from others how great it is!

The David Frost wine site utilizes several ways to sign people up for its newsletters and offers including a contest, a download, and a newsletter sign-up banner!

17. Let your visitors know how **many people have already subscribed to your ezine.** This suggests credibility and value.

18. If your ezine is of general interest, list it in all the **free ezine directories available.**

19. **Swap ads** with other ezine publishers to drive traffic to each other's publications.

20. If all else fails, **you can even buy subscribers** for your ezine through third-party companies. They offer a list of ezines available by type and drive traffic to the list. Visitors then select which of the free ezines they want and the third party bills you for each name.

Whatever you do to acquire email subscribers, treat them like the gold they are!

Having the power to distribute your message to a large number of people with the touch of a button is a marketing power you can't afford to ignore!

CHAPTER 56

Slicing and Dicing Your Database for Optimal Response!

Over the last five years a great many businesses have invested the time and effort it takes to build a large database of potential customers. Some even do a good job of contacting their database regularly by email. However, if that contact is not aimed at the right people, it will not only fail to generate business but it will quickly shrink your database in the process.

In today's market, you cannot send blanket emails to an unsorted list of prospects and customers and expect your message to resonate with a majority of the list. Yet this is exactly what most business owners do. Why? Because they don't have the technology to easily get a far better response from target mailings.

Call me sexist, but I couldn't care less about the "ladies' tennis" events that my club sends me, any more than I care about the "seniors early-bird dinner specials" at my local restaurant on Tuesdays! And, if you keep sending me stuff I'm not interested in, I'll unsubscribe!

So will YOU!

All data should be sorted into logical groups that make sense for your operation. For example, I sort my partners by industry, such as golf, travel, products, real estate, and so on.

Western-style riders are a very different equestrian breed than

English-style riders. If you're a company that services the Western market, that's an obvious division you would want to make with your marketing messages. At a car dealership or auto service center you would sort by car type. Bentley owners usually have a very different mindset than Ferrari owners. Ferrari owners are different than Porsche owners.

Targeting your various subgroups can be easily accomplished with Marketing Commander. Once you have your data sliced into logical groups, you can preprogram Marketing Commander to contact these groups automatically with up to a year's worth of targeted promotions for each group.

Every single promotion at your business, from a New Year's Eve party to the July 4th sales event, is preprogrammed and ready for an automatic and timely deployment to specific vertical lists! You do nothing! Marketing Commander sends a beautiful, customized email promotion out, at exactly the right time, whether YOU happen to be in your office or vacationing in Europe!

Even this is not enough in today's world to get maximum response. Today people want true one-to-one marketing with offers and content that speak to their individual wants and tastes.

One-to-One Marketing

Let's look at an example of true automated one-to-one marketing in action. Suppose a prospect has expressed an interest in a wine tasting event through an online survey, but it's only January and the event is not until May. Not to worry. Marketing Commander will AUTOMATICALLY follow-up with an email on a prescribed date, letting ONLY the visitors who answered "YES" to interest in wine tasting know the date and details of the event.

*While there may be other solutions that do everything
Marketing Commander does, if there are, I haven't found
them yet and trust me, I've been looking!*

Marketing Commander will follow-up again two weeks later (your choice of frequency) with more information and instructions so they can register online for the event!

Marketing Commander is even programmed to *not* send follow-up sales messages to those already registered. It's like having a full-time marketing staff inside your computer.

Now apply this concept to every event and service you offer at your business. By allowing people to indicate their preferences, you massively increase your chances of a positive response. People interested in social events or theme parties get invites while those who are not, don't. People interested in how-to information receive it, while those who don't like to read will not, making each group far more likely to respond to those offers that fit their interests!

So building a big database is still critical, but you also need to be able to slice and dice it. Your goal should be to take your offers down all the way to the individual preferences of the thousands of people in your database in order to maximize your response.

The true power of email marketing is making specific and relevant offers to people who have already indicated what they want!

CHAPTER 57

E-bolt Campaigns for Maximum Conversion of Leads to Sales!

E-bolts are individual emails in a series. E-bolts are not as effective as their Thunderbolt postal counterpart (see Chapter 20 on Thunderbolt Marketing). While not all emails get through or get read, e-bolt campaigns are still staggeringly more effective than how most businesses follow up on their leads. Using personalized autoresponder technology, you can follow up automatically three, ten, even twenty times or more depending on your product and sales cycle.

This form of marketing is ideal for high-priced products or services with a long decision time. It's ideal for professional services, real estate, schools, memberships, and high-end products of all kinds.

For example, say someone inquires about your real estate development in Florida. Let's look at what happens next.

1. Email goes out thanking the prospects for filling in the form and promising to send them more info in the mail (which you send via snail mail).

2. Email goes out with the highlights of the community and tells the prospect that there is so much to tell that you will be in touch with more info shortly.

3. Now you start to send emails about just one aspect of the community at a time. In this one you talk about the quality of the golf course.

4. In this one, you highlight fishing, bird watching, and nature.

5. In this one, talk about the nearby beaches and boating opportunities.

6. In this one, talk up the pool, spa, and health and fitness facilities in the development.

7. In this one, tell your prospects how friendly the neighbors will be. Include lots of testimonials from existing residents!

8. In this one, wax poetic about the beautiful Florida weather especially in the winter!

9. In this one, describe the social aspects of the golf, tennis, and community clubhouse.

10. In this one, highlight the new models you have coming online or the opportunities in re-sales.

11. In this one, showcase the shopping, concerts, and local culture.

12. In this one, tell them you are astonished you have not had the opportunity to meet them personally yet and ask if they are still interested? If they are, start a new campaign.

Emails are set to go weekly for the first few weeks, then change to monthly after the fourth or fifth. They can, of course, be personalized using the Marketing Commander technology. If the prospect does not fish, then you skip that email and send,

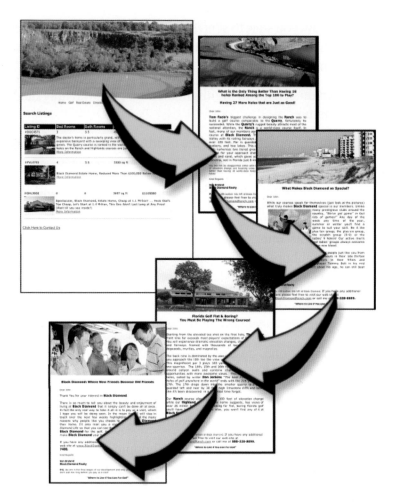

Sending multiple emails over time on the specific benefits of your product will dramatically increase sales.

instead, one about the local art scene because *that's* what they said they enjoyed in the survey.

Each email ends with a strong call to ACTION to get the prospect to actually visit the development! The difference in response between following up in this manner or following up in the traditional manner with a couple of letters and the odd phone call is staggering!

How Much Is Too Much Follow-Up?

Most people are very worried about following up in this fashion and they always ask how much is too much? There is no perfect answer to this question, but I'll say this: If someone is truly interested in your product or service, they will more than likely be glad you stayed in constant touch. If they are not, then they will click unsubscribe or let you know they are no longer interested!

You will lose far more money by NOT following up repeatedly than you ever will by overkill!

To see examples of real e-bolt campaigns for a variety of products and services go to:

www.CunninglyCleverMarketing.com

Make your follow up to all leads automatic, personalized, and relentless!

CHAPTER 58

Use In-Bound Emails as Sales Leads

I get way too much email — in excess of 1,000 a day. But hidden in all those subscriptions and even some of the spam are golden leads — you just have to look. I frequently use an in-bound email solicitation as the starting point of a relationship rather than just deleting it.

I might email back something that says:

> I got your email about your new land development in North Carolina but when I followed the link and got to your site I noticed several important tools missing to help you turn traffic into sales. My company Legendary Marketing specializes in lead generation using an amazing product for turning prospects into sales called Marketing Commander.
>
> Your property looks lovely, I hate to think how much money you are losing by not having these simple tools on your website.
>
> Please call me today at….

You'd be surprised how much business you can gain in this manner simply by tying your response into their outbound email.

Many inbound emails can be an opportunity to start a dialogue!

CHAPTER 59

An Embarrassingly Brilliant Mistake!

A couple of years ago I decided to try something cunningly clever with my ezine. I wrote an inbound question from a fictional client addressing all the problems a typical business faced with their marketing. In reply to the lengthy question, I wrote a cutting response in a way that suggested a personal relationship with him. I talked about how his boss had his hands tied and would spend $50,000 on this or that but not $5,000 on marketing. I also covered all the other usual problems I face when looking for new partners. Then I "accidently" sent it to my entire subscriber database.

The whole thing was in plain text just like a regular email and not like my regular newsletter. The response was phenomenal. While a number simply emailed me to tell me I had sent them the wrong email by mistake, many more wrote back to say they had very similar problems. This opened up dialogues that led to a ton of new business!

Here is an example of a follow-up campaign that, while still in a newsletter form, follows another fictional email exchange that was also tremendously successful.

From the Legend's Laptop
Currently located in my New Home on the 6th Hole of
The Ranch Course at Black Diamond Ranch!
www.LegendaryMarketing.com

Issue 13

The Alarming Tale of a Troubled Course Manager and His Struggle to Retain His Sanity!

Dear Reader:

And so it came to pass that I began to wonder, "How best to help my subscribers this month?" What morsel of information can I pass on that will help fill their coffers with the huge wads of cash of which they all seem uncommonly fond?

The answer came to me over my third cup of coffee in the form of an email from a prospective client.

Dear Mr. Wood:

I am the INSANE guy you keep talking about in all your communications. We keep lowering our green fees and reducing our membership fees. We run print ads that don't make the phone ring and provide our staff with no sales training, in case the phone did actually ring!

The woman we have in outing & membership sales is like the Wicked Witch of the West, but I'm scared to fire her because three of my members really like her, and it might cause problems. Mainly because one of them is a silent investor and I think she is … well … you know … on her side. (And it used to be the guys you worried about… eh?)

Our first website that my daughter's boyfriend

did for us for FREE was worthless, but I didn't
want to hurt her feelings, so I kept using it for
years. When I eventually switched, and, I'll be
honest with you, I was looking for something for
nothing, so I went with that guy in Texas who
copies all your emails the week after you run them.
I should have known better. I mean I have been
imitating my competitors for years, and where has
it gotten me? Right on the verge of bankruptcy -
that's where!

On a positive note, our graphics company won
an award for the brochures they designed for us,
although no one over 18 years old can seem to read
the 8-point font they so cleverly set in reverse
type to make it look nice. This is a bit of an
issue as most of our customers are over 50!

We invited a marketing consultant who I heard
at a convention around to lunch. (I should have
suspected something fishy when he showed up in a
used Yugo. Can't see you doing that, Mr. Wood.) He
said the problem was our brand. He said we needed
a new logo and a new image. He even suggested
switching the lunch menu to sushi to attract a
younger crowd, but to be honest it was a flop.
Especially after a member of the board ate the
wrong part of a blowfish and died. Quite tragic
really… and it was all over in 15 seconds. Even
without the blowfish incident, it's really a meat
and potato crowd here.

On the plus side, the course has a really
fantastic layout, designed by Jack Trent Dye. Even
though it's 8,500 yards from the tips, it's a very
enjoyable 7,400 from the ladies tees. Everyone
loves it although, strangely enough, we don't get
much repeat play!

With the exception of the bag drop, bar, dining
room, and the guy who takes tee times over the
phone, the service is really great and everyone

loves our cart girl, Dolly! (Except a couple of the stuffier female members; I mean let's be fair, it's not her fault that cheap Chinese cotton shrinks with every wash!)

Based on your newsletter suggestions, we have worked hard to come up with a new USP for the 2009 season.

"A Great Layout and Great Service!"

What do you think?

I am hoping that it can really set us apart from the other 50 clubs in our market! Although I must admit a couple have similar Unique Selling Propositions like "Committed to an Excellent Golf Experience" and the club right across the street is "Experience Excellent Golf and Service!" But I think ours is clearly superior and likely to make a strong statement in the market.

Speaking of making a statement, I took the advice from one of your newsletters last year and made an IRRESISTIBLE offer to prospective new members. It resulted in over $275,000 in new business at a cost of just $20,000! However, I have decided not to do it again this year, because it seems to me that if I do it every year, they will come to expect irresistible offers. So I went back to the "pay before January 31st and we will discount your membership by 2.75%" approach! I upped it from a 1.75% discount by a full point to make it "sexier." However, as in 2008, not a single person responded to the offer!

Well, Mr. Wood, I have taken enough of your incredibly valuable time. Do you have any advice that you think will help me have a better year in 2006?

Yours Insanely,

Dr. Richard Cranium

MY RESPONSE to the Good Doctor's Unique Situation

Dear Dr. Cranium:

Indeed, I do.

Don't do the same things you have always done and expect different results.

TAKE THE FOLLOWING ACTIONS IMMEDIATELY:

1) Read the *Golf Marketing Bible* over the holidays. If you have not ordered the *Golf Marketing Bible* yet, do it now. Go To www.TheGolfMarketingBible.com.

2) Attend the Golf Marketing Boot Camp in January.

3) Switch to **Golf Marketing Commander** -- the ultimate golf website and marketing tool.

If you do just these three things your problems will be over, your income will rise, and your insanity will be cured.

All the Best,
Andrew Wood
Marketing Legend

P.S. Have a Wonderful Christmas and Happy and Prosperous New Year. We are always here to help!

Invent your own fictional customer with problems to solve. Then have some fun answering his questions!

CHAPTER 60

How I Made $75,000 in Three Days from an 11-Page Email No One Read!

I keep reading that people won't read any more, that they want their information in sound bites like on CNN, that your web and email copy should be short or it will be ignored. So I guess it should have come as no surprise to me that none of the 60 plus people in the room, who had come to my Marketing Boot Camp and paid $1,595 to do so, had read my 11-page email.

Certainly when I asked if anyone would read an 11-page email no one put their hands up! Some people actually chuckled at the thought, as they shook their heads knowingly.

But then something strange happened!

I pointed out that the only way I had advertised the marketing boot camp was via an 11-page email. They exchanged nervous glances, "Well, YES! We read that?" they said in muffled voices.

"Why?" I asked.

"Because you promised to increase our bottom line by $50,000 to $250,000. Because you addressed a bunch of the issues we face and promised practical solutions. Because you offered a triple money-back guarantee if we did not think it was the most valuable seminar we had EVER been to!" they chimed.

"So did you read the entire letter before committing to spend $1,595 plus airfare, hotel, and rental car?" I persisted.

About 95% of them admitted they had and at least a dozen said they read through the email several times before committing!

NO one had not read the majority of the 11 pages!

The fact that you are using email as your media does not mean you can get away without making a REAL sales pitch if you want to get results! People still want enticing headlines, real benefits, testimonials, guarantees, calls to action, and irresistible offers. They still have to be sold!

To read the entire 11-page email go to:

www.CunninglyCleverMarketing.com

The more you tell, the more you sell!

Don't believe anyone who says otherwise. Even if it's email!

CHAPTER 61

Email Response and Conversion Rates

Recently I was asked for perhaps the thousandth time: What is a typical response to an email campaign?

The truth is, there is NO typical response; each one is different. I have sent 3,000,000 emails containing an astonishing book promotion to the entire list I own and gotten just 80 sales. I have also emailed 500 people a free golf offer and gotten 1,580 responses!

YES, 1,580 and in just 48 hours!

First we must ask how good is the data. At best, about 50% of any rented data will be good; people change emails, move companies, and so forth.

Then we must ask how much gets through because of spam filters, firewalls, blocked IP's, etc. Let's say 30% of the remaining 50% gets through.

Then we must ask how much gets opened from a blind mailing. It's usually less than 1% for rented lists. Even in most 100% opt-in lists, where recipients were registered at the site from which the mailing comes so they are familiar with the company, the open rates are generally between 15–35%.

Then you have to consider the offer, current weather, day the mailing was sent, and 100 other things.

But also consider this, if I mail 100,000 people in the Northeast information on a Florida real estate community and ask them to register for more information, I will get between 80 and 150 leads in less than a week. On the surface, that's an astonishingly bad response as a percentage. But if we use the universal 80/20 rule, that's still 15–30 qualified leads in a week. How many developments are doing that these days?

How qualified are they?

As qualified as the questions you ask.

FOCUS not on the numbers you email but on the QUALITY of your leads and the QUALITY of your follow up once the lead is generated.

In Dallas I blasted an offer to 5,000 golfers on my list; 140 filled in my 20 questions. Next I rented a list from a third party and blasted an additional 21,000 names — 104 more people signed up. Then we made the same offer to a third rental list and finally we ran an ad in the newspaper. Total names and 20-question surveys generated in a couple of weeks — over 700 so far. This represents a response rate well below 1%, but the course has spent about $3000 and now, including names gathered at the counter, has a 1,000 player e-list in just three weeks! What's more, they also have numerous membership, banquet, and outing leads as well!

If you understand marketing at all, you understand that acquiring a new customer for $3 and finding 20 of his/her preferences before he even walks in the door may be the best business bargain on the planet! Even if it were $50 a customer, this might be the most cost-effective and trackable campaign this club does all year!

FOCUS on great follow up with people who respond to your email offers and don't worry about the 5.6 billion who don't!!

CHAPTER 62

Quick Start to Major Profits!

The fastest way to email success, other than the continually mentioned strategy of building your own huge opt-in database, is to rent data and embark on a multistep campaign. It's important that you commit to a multi-step campaign because hitting a home run with one e-blast is rare!

Anatomy of a successful e-marketing campaign:

- Rent 100,000 emails of people in New York and New Jersey who play golf.

- Send a blast in late Fall inviting them to take a discounted discovery trip at a specific Florida development by registering on the development website.

- 180 say yes; thank them by email at once.

- Send discovery kit in the mail the next day.

- Follow up with 12-step auto e-bolt campaign.

- Follow up with 7-letter Thunderbolt campaign.

- Follow up with multiple scripted phone calls to get them to commit to a date.

- Have a scripted sales process and orchestrated discover tour in place when they come.

- Train staff in the execution of both.

- Sales beat expectations; blast another 100,000!

- Ask buyers for specific referrals!

We repeated this process two more times before the response fell off from this list source.

**If you will make the commitment to e-market
in the systematic way I described above,
you will be astonished how much more effective
your marketing will be!**

7

Cunningly Clever Sales Letters

CHAPTER 63

It's Hard to Beat Old-Fashioned Direct Mail

Over the last decade I have made the majority of my income from the Internet. One of my companies, Marketing Commander, sells the world's leading marketing website software. So it often surprises people when I tell them that the most effective form of marketing is, in fact, good old-fashioned direct mail.

Marketing Effectively by Mail

Over the last few months I have been on a quest to gather marketing materials from every high-end golf real estate development in the country, plus a number outside the country. This is partly because I am looking for a second home and partly because I just wanted to see how BAD most marketing really is when orchestrated by traditional ad agencies.

I have samples of oversized leather-bound brochures, hardcover books masquerading as brochures, and multimedia packages with DVDs, videos, and the kitchen sink enclosed. Plus just about every imaginable variation of glossy stock and slick brochure. All cost tens of thousands of dollars to produce and as much as $5 each to mail!

Millions of dollars in printing and mailing and not ONE decent sales letter!

About the only thing I don't have in over 100 examples (see picture) is a DECENT sales letter, NOT ONE!!

Every package has poor or non-existent headlines, with no story, NO testimonials, no call to action, and only about three good offers out of a hundred. Over ten million dollars worth of marketing down the proverbial drain — but — you know what I bet?

I bet they won some awards!!

Here is another observation that you can only really appreciate if you look at a dozen packages or more (exactly the type of twisted thing a real prospect might actually do!)

All these high-end "vision" brochures look and sound EXACTLY the same. I can't tell from reading their VISION if the property is located in North Carolina, Utah, Colorado, California, or Timbuktu!

Some developments even use the very same stock art!

NONE TELL THE REAL STORY of **THEIR** DEVELOPMENT, with PASSION, although many of them have GREAT stories just crying out to be told!!!

Direct mail is the most effective form of marketing for most types of business, but getting a GREAT response is far more about crafting a good sales letter than it is about spending $100,000 on photos, printing, and mailing.

YOU ONLY have to succeed once in writing a KILLER sales letter. It will cost you about 90% less than the TYPICAL ad agency campaign. You'll be converted to this form of marketing for life!

Nothing will make your company more money than a great sales letter sent to the right people. NOTHING!

CHAPTER 64

Why You Should Go to Ridiculous Lengths to Handcraft Your Prospect Mailing List…If You Actually Want an Astonishing Response to Your Mailings!

There is an old saying that "close only works in horseshoes and hand grenades." Nowhere is that more true than in picking the right people to target with your marketing.

The need to develop a great list is information that few people want.

Few people want it because it involves painstaking, mind-numbing, WORK!

Everyone wants the quick and easy solution, so they buy giant directories or mailing lists of magazine subscribers, new homeowners, or dubious "prospect" names from third-party vendors. **All of these solutions are a start but that's all they are. Most are suited only as the first step in building a list**

of REAL PROSPECTS, not for actually making a direct sale. If you try to circumvent this FACT, you will almost always be disappointed.

The success of almost all Cunningly Clever campaigns goes back, first and foremost, to spending a great deal of time and effort in defining your target market and building a great prospect list.

Here is a thought. Instead of spending $25,000 buying a list, then printing and mailing to 25,000 people who you *think*, because of a single criteria or two, might buy your company's product or service, spend $5,000 on building a GREAT list of 500 QUALIFIED prospects FIRST. **People who are willing to put their hands in the air and be counted.** Then mail to those 500 people seven times.

The response will be a thousand percent greater and you won't spend a dime more that you budgeted in the first place. In fact, you'll spend a great deal less!

This is still a hard concept for most people to grasp because almost everyone is seduced by the law of large numbers. But 100,000 people seeing your ad does not guarantee any success! In fact, it does not even guarantee a phone call!

Since most people really don't track their ads, most don't know for sure how little response most print ads generate.

You MUST START by COMMITING the time and resources to HANDCRAFT your PROSPECT LIST. Success in this endeavor is measured in quality NOT quantity!

First, decide what your specific written criteria will be for inclusion in your mailing list. The tougher the criteria, the better!

Once you have determined your exact criteria, you will use a variety of methods to qualify prospects into your final mailing list until you reach your desired number of prospects for the campaign.

The first secret to massive response from your mailing, no matter what your business or product, is to pay attention to list quality, not list quantity!

CHAPTER   65

Building Your Million-Dollar Mailing List in Six Weeks or Less!

It's not difficult to build a million-dollar mailing list. Anyone can do it; it just takes time and effort. Start by combing your computer, desk, files, and pockets for all existing data. Even though it might not be current, it can at least be re-qualified by mail or phone quickly.

Look at your local media every day; it is swimming with leads. Make your website the focus of all of your prospecting efforts. Use ads, direct mail, radio, TV, and e-blasts to drive people to a contact point on your website where they will express an interest in your products and services. Entice prospects to register with contests, offers, emails, free stuff, DVDs, audios, green fees, room nights, newsletters, special reports, and e-clubs.

Local discussion groups and industry chat rooms are another great source of prospects. Scan them regularly and make posts that direct people back to your website with the offer of free information.

Don't forget the obvious: existing clients, past clients, referrals, trade show leads, and vendors. Look for alliances with non-competing companies to quickly enhance your prospect list by sharing data.

Use telemarketing to qualify new prospects in your area, re-qualify old lists, and to add an additional layer of quality to new lists. If you outsource the job, it's painless and can usually be accomplished in a couple of weeks or less!

Many companies have large files of people with whom they have done business in the past, sometimes the very distant past. Most of them also have decent numbers of people who have inquired but never bought. Then there are the various Excel spreadsheets handed down from previous employees, the origin and make-up of which are long since lost. Add to that file drawers full of handwritten notes, business cards from long-forgotten trade shows, and a rolodex no one ever bothered to digitize. You'll have a perfect source of great leads, just as soon as you call them all and re-qualify these multiple sources into a single quality mailing list.

Finally, look for people of influence who can plug you into their networks, as well as the occasional dream contact. The dream contact is the one contact who, if you got them to buy, would bring with them an avalanche of other business.

Let me stress again most STRONGLY — spending a few thousand dollars to get this end of your house in order will be worth 100 times the money you waste on mailing greater quantities of poorer quality names. The target list of quality prospects that you build and eventually contact seven times or more will be much more valuable.

Spend time, money, and effort building a great list before you ever mail to anyone!

CHAPTER 66

Send Cunningly Clever Sales Letters to Old Lists to Uncover Real Prospects

Here is a wonderful example of a letter designed to get people **to put their hands in the air and be counted as REAL prospects.** Seventy-eight meeting planners responded to this letter sent to an old list of just over 800 meeting planners taken from a directory.

Ashley Langley, Lewiston, Mi

Hi Barry:

My Name is Ashley and I could sure use your help!

That's my picture in case you wonder what I look like. I know I always wonder when I get letters from people I don't know.

I just took a new job working for Garland Resort. I'm sure you have probably heard of them because they are Michigan's most beautiful resort. Anyway, I am pretty new at this and they told me to be innovative. While I am training, I thought <u>I'd</u> <u>send you a letter and see if you could help me show</u> <u>my boss that even though I am young I have good</u> <u>ideas.</u>

I just read this great marketing book by Andrew Wood. He said the very first thing you have to do to be successful in marketing is to identify people who might want to buy your product. So I got this list of meeting planners from a big book, which is why I am writing to you.

You see, I don't know if the meeting space at Garland is right for you or your organization. That's why I sent a card along with this letter to see if you would ever consider Garland as a location for one of your IMPORTANT meetings.

PLEASE SEND this card back as I paid for all the stamps with my own money.

Thank you for helping me and for your valuable time. I know if this works, my boss will be very pleased.

Yours sincerely,

Ashley Langley

P.S. I heard them talking the other day about this really neat new program they are offering for every meeting attendee. It's a free, take-home, self-study Leadership program. It's got a neat manual, 12 audio CDs and it's worth $595. It's by Andrew Wood the same guy who wrote the marketing book I read, so I would think it's really good! It's sort of like getting two meetings for the price of one and I figure everyone wants leadership skills. I know I do.

You can check it out at:

www.GarlandInstitute.com

It's worth mailing letters to qualify your list before you mail them multiple times with your real offer!

CHAPTER 67

A Short But Critical Course in How Prospects Sort Mail!

When a prospect gets a letter from you in the mail, the VERY FIRST CHALLENGE you have is *not* to get him to read your headline or respond to your exciting offer — it's far more IMPORTANT than that!

The REAL challenge is to get your prospect to PLACE YOUR letter on the interesting pile!

Fail to do that and I don't care what you spent or what you sent, or for that matter, who wrote your copy, your campaign is DOOMED!

Have you ever watched someone open the mail?

It's a very interesting study in human nature and, interestingly, almost always happens in close vicinity to a wastepaper basket or recycling can!

Take me for example, I'm a sorter.

First I look through the stack for checks and bills. That's **Pile A — the accounting pile.**

Pile B is the family pile — This is anything for my wife or children, horse magazines, girl catalogs, or video game offers.

Just about everyone sorts their mail before opening it. Your goal is to avoid your mailing pieces ending up on the "toss pile."

Pile C is the "later pile" — This pile includes catalogs that might be of potential interest (golf, car stuff, and at Christmas at least, possible gifts for my wife) and periodicals. They get put on my magazine rack for later reading at night or for my next plane trip.

Pile D is interesting stuff — This one is my favorite. It's the interesting stuff — a handwritten letter from a friend, books or CDs I ordered, brochures for interesting vacations, and direct mail offers for things that interest me (books, audios, cars, golf, and so forth).

Which brings me to…

Pile E — Pile E is direct mail offers that *might* be of interest to me. Only pile E almost never exists because very few pieces make it through the sort-and-trash process. I dump letters from Oprah and Bill Clinton (we were never that close anyway). I dump credit card offers, sweepstakes, insurance solicitations, and local car dealer letters straight in trash. No, I don't want a Buick and I never will, even if Tiger Woods drives one. (Please — Tiger wouldn't be caught dead in a Buick. The last time I checked he actually drove a Twin Turbo Porsche. Heck, his henchmen won't even drive the Buicks he gives them!)

Anyway, I am sure you get the point. For sure, there are other methods of sorting your mail, but they all have one thing in common, some stuff gets thrown out without a glance, some gets saved for later reading, and some actually gets OPENED and READ!

Make sure you take steps to get your mail placed in the "open" pile rather than the round file!

CHAPTER 68

20 Proven Techniques to Massively Increase the Chance Your Mail Gets Opened and Read!

A brilliant sales letter is a complete waste if your envelope never gets opened. Here are 20 tried-and-tested techniques to get your prospects and customers to open your envelopes:

1. **Use a colored envelope** or use an envelope with an unusual shape or design that will make it jump out from the masses of white, commercial number tens.

2. **Use large envelopes** such as 6 1/2 by 9 1/2 inches, or even 9 by 12 inches. This is expensive, but the envelope will be opened.

3. **Use an unusual material for the envelope**, say vellum or a textured paper. In tests conducted by a paper merchant, this alone increased responses significantly. The additional revenue generated by the mailing more than compensated for the additional cost for the special paper.

4. **Use an official looking envelope.** Letters that look like they come from an official agency or authoritative source get more response.

An unusual envelope will increase the odds it will be opened.

5. **Use window envelopes.** Window envelopes can be good especially if the prospect can see something interesting through the envelope.

6. Another good technique (albeit considerably more expensive) when targeting upper-level executives is to **send your sales letter or direct mail package via Federal Express.** Recent surveys of executives on the topic of what gets opened and what gets read indicate that FedEx gets the job done. FedEx envelopes get past gatekeepers and into the hands of those you want to reach.

   While on the surface this may seem like a huge investment, if you are only mailing a few hundred to a very targeted group, it may well pay off. Perhaps, use this method to get your first package in their hands then follow up through more traditional channels. When you consider the cost of a membership, outing, home or vacation it may well pay off because you know that NONE of your competitors would be so bold as to test this method.

7. **Hand address your envelopes.** Okay, so you are not going to sit down and address 500 envelopes by hand, but the cart girl wanting to make some extra money might. Failing that, call a temp agency or post a notice on a college bulletin board. *Few people will make the extra effort, but that effort will produce better results!*

8. **Do not use mailing labels.** If you can't hand address, use an ink-jet printer to print the address directly onto the envelope.

9. **Use blue ink instead** of black to address your letters or if you must use labels, use colored labels to help your letters stand out from the crowd.

10. **Make sure you get the prospect's name and title correct.** How do you feel when sales people or telemarketers mispronounce your name? Your prospects feel the same way when your letter arrives with their name or initials misspelled or their title incorrect. As bad as my spelling normally is, I make a special effort with names. (People get real touchy about this.)

11. **Use a real stamp** not a prepaid or postage paid indicia. Preferably a nice commemorative stamp.

12. **Get your own stamp** — like we now have using our own Legendary Marketing logo — it's legal now! This is obviously far more expensive than going bulk,

but it's also far more effective so you must weigh the cost against the return.

13. **If you have to use a meter, use first class postage** at least on your first mailing, so you get the returns.

To Tease or Not to Tease, That is the Question

There has always been a big debate in direct marketing circles about whether or not to put teaser copy on the outside of the envelope. The idea, of course, is to tease them with the contents of your letter in a strong enough way to get them to open it.

The down side to this is that they know now that the letter is in fact a solicitation for something. So which works better — the art of disguise or the art of persuasion? The truth is, both methods can work, it really depends on the type of campaign you are running and who your specific target audience happens to be.

14. **First, the disguised letter.** When you're attempting to create a first-class, personal letter look, do not use teaser copy or a mailing label. It flags your piece as advertising. If there's no writing on the envelope, the reader HAS to open it in order to check out the contents.

15. **The opposite strategy is to treat your outer envelope like a billboard.** When you take the "billboard" approach, you make no attempt to disguise the fact that your mail is advertising mail. As the name implies, using this technique means that you treat your envelope as a billboard — actually printing "teaser copy" on the outside of the envelope. The objective of your teaser copy is to get your prospect to think: "Hmm, I ought to take a look at this."

Here are some examples of effective teaser copy:

- Your Invitation to Membership Enclosed

- Free Room and an Upgrade. Details Inside

- Free DVD to Lower Your Scores

- Free Report on Retiring in Florida

- Invitation to VIP Event...enclosed

Interestingly, simply printing "OPEN NOW" often works.

Don't give away too much information. The sole objective of your teaser copy is to get your mail opened. So don't give away too much information on the outer envelope. The element of intrigue is very important. If the prospects think they understand your offer, there's no incentive to open the envelope. Your teaser should "tease." Make the reader open the envelope to get the full offer and story.

Envelope design and teaser copy should follow the very same headline and copy rules outlined in this manual. The teaser is the *ad* for your sales letter.

The envelope design should reflect the image of the product and the audience it's being targeted to. Don't shout when you should whisper. Don't be white-collar when you should be blue-collar. Don't be formal when you should be informal, and so on.

Teaser copy/graphics should promise or reflect a user benefit whether expressed or implied.

To do this, you can use any number of techniques described in previous modules including:

- Ask questions you know the prospect can relate to and that imply a benefit.

- Use testimonials that express a real benefit.

- Announce something NEW or FREE.

- List a series of benefits.

- Use a headline similar to one you would write for a publication ad.

- Start the first paragraph of your letter on the envelope, stop it at a key point and continue on the sales letter.

16. **Involvement devices on envelopes.** Extra windows exposing tokens, peel-and-stick labels, side opening envelopes, and the like can improve your "opening percentage."

17. **The return address does not have to be there.** Did you know that the only time postal regulations require you to include identification on the envelope is when you're mailing at the low rates available to fundraisers only? With no return address, a good percentage of people will open the envelope just to see who it's from.

19. **Use a more personal or interesting return address** rather than just your business name and address. For example:

From the Desk of Andrew Wood
Marketing Legend

or

From the Desk of Barry Owens
Golf Outing Czar

or

Celebrities can attract attention to your letter.

Important Information from The Law Office of
Dewey, Screwem & Howe

19. **USE VARIETY.** People tire of seeing the same envelope month after month. If they have thrown it away once, they will throw it away again. So put your sales message inside a variety of different envelopes. Use the space on the back of the envelope to encourage the prospects to OPEN your letter. A lot of the envelopes I see completely ignore the back surface. This can be a huge mistake. You see, you never know how your package is going to fall on someone's desk. That's why it makes good sense to use both sides of the envelope if your printing budget permits.

20. **Test different envelope copy and graphics** (and no teaser/graphic envelopes) just as you would any other

component of a package. There can be significant differences in response.

Cracker Jack Box Trinkets Catch Big Fish

Add a tee, pencil, magnet, or some other lumpy trinket inside the letter to create some interest. I have used everything from ball markers to tea bags to seed packets to divots! They are not going to trash that letter like the rest of the "junk mail!" They are going to first put it on the interesting pile.

Be careful — the post office has very tricky rules about what you can send at regular first-class rates. Odd-sized envelopes or "lumpy" envelopes pay a higher first-class rate.

Adopt one of these Cunningly Clever ideas to make sure your mail gets read!

CHAPTER 69

The Lost Art of Storytelling: Connecting with Your Readers!

A great many businesses rely heavily on good old-fashioned sale letters to drum up business. A great many more rely on sales letters to seal the deal after a prospect has expressed interest by phone or through the Internet. The problem is that good "old fashioned" letters don't work the way they used to in this modern world.

Now don't get me wrong, a great sales letter may still be the best marketing money can buy, but it has to be great! Not a fill-in-the-blank John Doe letter that, apart from your company name, could be done by your 50 closest competitors. Look at the letters you get from Realtors, insurance brokers, and other such service providers. They're almost identical. They're killing trees with worthless letters that often hit the trash without even being read!

People Love Stories!

Since time began, man has loved stories. They painted them on walls of caves before they had the words to speak them. They tell stories around campfires, at pubs, and at 19th holes around the world. They sing them in songs and write them in books. The best stories are handed down from generation to generation, embellished and re-told. They often live on for hundreds, sometimes even thousands, of years beyond their origins.

This is true of every culture on planet earth. Yet it's very often overlooked by slick marketing people who are obsessed with style and image over substance and results!

The story should be the heart of your sales letter. It's what you build your headlines, benefits, and offers around. It's the glue that makes everything else stick.

If you can take your basic marketing message and wrap it in a compelling story, you can produce astonishingly better results from your marketing!

Where do you look for great stories for your company?

1. **Use personal stories** from your business and life.

2. **Think of stories, feedback, and comments you have gathered from customers and clients.**

3. **How is your product made?** What makes it different?

4. **What is your company's history?** Who started it and why? What's the story behind the story?

5. **What is your organization passionate about?**

6. If you can't find anything within, **draw your story from popular culture.**

7. **Look outside your particular industry** at the various marketing you get from every available source.

8. If you can't find stories from any other source, make them up!

Choose your core story and write it out. Try to do it in less than 12 lines of text. Make it interesting, make it memorable, and make it speak to your reader.

This information is just as true when writing web copy, brochure copy, or movie scripts!

For some great examples visit:

www.cunninglyclevermarketing.com/storyletters

The power of a great story in producing superior results for your marketing cannot be overstated.

CHAPTER 70

$1,742 in Actual Sales per Letter Mailed!

From The Desk of Barry Owens
Golf Outing Czar
Garland Resort

I AM GOING TO MAKE YOU AN OFFER
YOU CAN'T REFUSE!

I'm Going to Send You Swimming with the Manatees!

Dear Wally:

Recently I watched the movie *The Godfather,* which I haven't seen in 20 years, hence my catchy headline...

BUT I THINK WHEN YOU Hear WHAT I HAVE to offer, you won't need a gun to your head to say YES to booking your golf outing at Garland ... Oh, and don't get me wrong about swimming with the manatees, it's a good thing, REALLY!

You see, I just hooked up with an old buddy who happens to run the **Plantation Inn Golf Resort**, located about an hour North of Tampa, Florida with easy access from the airport or I-75. It's a classic Florida layout that was once on the PGA tour and it has superior accommodations right on the banks of the famed Crystal River. The Crystal River is home to world-class fishing, boating and, of course, swimming with the manatees.

<u>Come on, think about it, what could be more fun than splashing around with a 1200-pound sea cow?</u>

Okay, lots of things, but seriously, people come from all over the world to do it and pay upwards of $300 a night to stay at the Plantation Inn. Not so you, my friend, because <u>one of the gifts I have for you, as part of the $3,000 gift package I have for booking your 2007 Golf Outing at Garland, is a three day, three night, three rounds of golf (FOR TWO) Plantation Inn Vacation worth $1500</u>. Plus $1500 in other prizes!!!

I only have 20 of these available so call now 866-617-2411 it's a great winter getaway and the famed World Woods is only 10 minutes away.

Regards,

Barry Owens
Golf Outing Czar

> **P.S.** Call now **866-617-2411** for Free golf and rooms in the Florida sun for two, plus $1500 in additional golf gifts — manatee not included!

You may like this letter or you may hate it. You may get it or you may not. Either way it was sent to 1,148 hand-picked people and generated $128,726 in actual bookings. Add in the food and beverage sales, plus resort spending and we are talking over $200,000 which works out to $1,742 per sales letter, give or take a few cents!

It works because it's written specifically to generate response from the particular target audience. It tells a story and makes an irresistible offer!

Grab the reader's attention, tell them a story, make them an irresistible offer.

Simple, effective, and VERY profitable!

CHAPTER 71

The Seven-Million-Dollar Sales Letter — Are You Insane?

Imagine a single-page sales letter that has worked for twenty years, in numerous different industries, to make me over seven million dollars, and my partners countless millions more! It has sold subscriptions, franchises, advertising, hotel rooms, consulting, seminars, club memberships, vacations, and real estate, to name just a few things, all with more or less the exact same letter, customized to that industry!

ARE YOU INSANE?

Dear Joe:

Now you may think that's a rather aggressive start to a letter from someone you don't even know, but bear with me and I promise that before you're ready to PUNCH ME IN THE FACE, I will explain.

First, allow me to ask you a few simple questions about the golf market in your area?

Has competition for business in your area gotten increasingly tough in recent seasons?

Are you SICK and TIRED of DISCOUNTS and FALLING profits?

Are you frustrated with your company's LACK of marketing success?

Are you secretly wondering how you're going to drive more business, sell product, or book business this year?

Now, I have just one more question: <u>What are you planning to do differently this season to turn your company on its ass and outsmart, outmarket, and outsell every single business in your industry?</u>

The reason I ask this last question is simple. Albert Einstein, who I'm sure you will agree was a pretty smart guy, had a very interesting definition of insanity. His definition of insanity was "doing the same thing over and over again and yet expecting different results!"

Doing the same things over and over again is exactly what all your competitors will be doing this season. They will be running the same old ads in the industry trade journals or regional style publications that they ran last year. They will be running the same discount offers and coupons in the local paper. They will be promoting the same worthless website and hoping that this year people will discover it! They might as well spend their entire marketing budget on lotto tickets!

There can ONLY be one WINNER in any market and I want it to be YOU!

In every market, in every part of the business, one company does better than all the rest! Usually it's the business that's partnered with Legendary Marketing. We are the world's leader in response marketing. We drive customers, participation, and profits, **guaranteed or your money back!**

 To learn more about how you can generate explosive growth for your business visit
                          or call **800 827 1663** now!

Sincerely,

Andrew Wood

 PS. For a FREE copy of our audio seminar **How to Generate Explosive Growth for Your Company, or The 12 Indisputable Laws of Marketing, call 800 827 1663** or request your FREE CD at www. LegendaryMarketing.com.

Why does this letter work so astonishingly well across industries, across countries, and across decades? I'll let you in on the secret, because it taps into a mindset that most people are ready and willing to buy into.

Whatever your customers are doing right now is not working the way they want it to. If it was, they wouldn't be reading your message!

CHAPTER 72

Thunderbolt Marketing — The World's Most Devastatingly Effective Marketing Strategy

I told you earlier that's there is nothing better to boost your business than a great sales letter, but that's not quite true. There is one thing: A series of seven great sales letters mailed in quick succession! A technique I have been using for over twenty years that I call Thunderbolt Marketing! Nothing I have ever done has produced more astonishing results.

1.8 Million Dollars from Just 198 Names

My first Thunderbolt campaign was in the karate business, aimed at 198 martial arts school owners. It was an attempt to get them to re-flag their schools from "Joe's Karate" to my franchise. NO easy task in that EGO-driven world, let me assure you!

Each of these prospects was handpicked based on how many students they had, how much they said they grossed, and various referrals from others in the industry. This information was gathered from written surveys and from telephone interviews. We had the added benefit of owning a magazine, *Martial Arts Business Magazine* (a complete exercise in self-promotion) that helped us leverage the information. In short, we knew that every one of the 198 targeted prospects should fit nicely into our program.

Sending a series of postcards is a cheap and effective way to execute Thunderbolt marketing campaign.

The Thunderbolt campaign generated 1.8 million dollars in income at a cost of less than $1,500 in printing and mailing. If you had to throw in the cost of gathering the information and creative design, you could still call it under $15,000. What makes this even more amazing is that there was no real offer, just lots of reasons to re-flag.

97 Responses from 900 Speakers Bureaus

When I started speaking to mainstream audiences on sales and marketing, I simply bought a list of the 900 speakers bureaus I could find at the time — not the best way to do it but I lacked time, not money. I mailed multiple postcards to all of them. Within a couple of weeks 97 came back as YES, we are interested; send us your speaking kit. (It is almost unheard of for speakers bureaus to request kits as they are inundated with wannabe speakers!)

$1.7 Million from 1,142 Names in Just 3 Months!

My all-time ROI champion is my **Garland Golf Outing Czar** Thunderbolt campaign. A related letter is given above.) This campaign, a mega-success by any measure, was aimed at golfers who had expressed an interest in holding a golf event at a resort. They had either previously held an event at the resort, called and asked about holding an event, or filled in a contact point on the website that said they would be interested. In all ways it was a targeted crowd. We did a typical Thunderbolt campaign with seven letters mailed in seven weeks with an irresistible offer (which discounted nothing)!

- In year one we had 398 people on our mailing list and generated $495,000 in bookings.

- In year two we had 600 people on our mailing list and generated $698,000 in bookings.

- In year three we had 900 people on our mailing list and generated $1.3 million in bookings.

- In year four we had 1,142 people on our mailing list and did $1.7 million in bookings.

Now those numbers are just rooms and golf. If you add in the on-site spending for food, drink, and other items, you are looking at $2.7 million this year from a Thunderbolt campaign that cost $20,000! A response so huge my meager math skills can't even begin to calculate the return on investment!

Getting to the Top Quickly

A campaign to 28 TOP CEOs in the manufacturing industry generated four inbound calls from the CEOs themselves and led to face-to-face appointments with three, even though they had never heard of the person or company who sent them the Thunderbolt campaign.

Thunderbolt Marketing can put YOU and YOUR company or club on the map no matter how big or small your prospects!

Building a Multi-Million Dollar Company from Scratch, with Nothing But a Thunderbolt Campaign

In building Legendary Marketing from the front room of my Florida home into a multimillion dollar company with over 300 clients and 40 employees in just 5 years, I went 60 months without printing a brochure of any kind!

That's right — the entire success of my advertising agency and my Internet company is based on Thunderbolt marketing.

I hit targeted prospects with good old-fashioned sales letters again and again. And remember, I am selling a high-tech product. Marketing Commander websites are the most technologically advanced in the industry — proof that Thunderbolt marketing can work in any industry, for any product!

I could give you hundreds more examples of how Thunderbolt marketing has worked for my clients and myself in as many different markets as you can imagine.

Thunderbolt marketing turns dead leads into gold. Let's face it — most organizations do a terrible job of following up on leads new or old. A few letters are exchanged, a few calls attempted, and then it goes in the dead pile perhaps without having ever reached the person.

With Thunderbolt marketing you can take an old list of prospects, ex-customers, or marginal customers and turn a surprising number of DEAD LEADS into sales, BIG sales!

At the very least you can reactivate their interest in what you have to offer by **getting them to call YOU!** When you can generate a substantial number of inbound calls instead of chasing leads, the whole dynamic of the sales process changes in YOUR FAVOR!

Thunderbolt marketing will instantly increase your top-of-the-mind awareness in your marketplace and create untold opportunities not related to your initial mailings for years to come. Because of the unique nature of the Thunderbolt approach, your prospects will talk about and pass around your materials to others in the area **creating a viral effect from your mailings, often doubling or tripling your circle of prospects.** This gives you a corresponding increase in response, sales, and profits!

No More Cold Calls — Prospects Will Seek You Out

Thunderbolt marketing works amazingly well in opening closed doors. You'll suddenly find it easy getting calls and appointments from CEOs, doctors, managers, and the top, hardest-to-reach people in every industry and every city.

In fact, you will never have to cold sell anything again.

PROSPECTS will be calling you asking about memberships, products, or whatever you sell!

That, of course, is the whole point of Thunderbolt marketing — to **maximize your time and efforts by getting people to pick up the phone and track you down** rather than the other way around!

You'll enjoy unexpected results as well, as you find people commenting on your company's creativity, ingenuity, and persistence. All fine traits to enhance your existing reputation in the marketplace.

For examples of highly effective Thunderbolt campaigns, go to:

www.CunninglyCleverMarketing.com

The only strategy more effective at producing astonishing response than a great sales letter is seven great sales letters sent in quick succession to a handcrafted list!

8

Marketing as Entertainment

CHAPTER 73

The Fine and Profitable Art of Entertaining Prospects While You Pitch Them!

How would you like your business's marketing material to be passed around the entire town, county, state — and perhaps even country?

For FREE!

How would you like free newspaper, radio, and even TV coverage? How would you like your entire database of current customers to become **instant evangelists for your marketing message?**

Sounds like some good ideas, right? But, before I tell you how you can accomplish such lofty goals and before I outline some of the cunningly clever marketing strategies that you might employ, let me start by asking you a few questions:

- Why do people buy magazines?

- Why do people go to websites?

- Why do people join clubs?

- Why do people buy books, listen to radio shows, and watch TV?

I'll tell you why: Entertainment!

Sure, a reasonable number of web surfers and magazine readers are looking for information, directions, or cooking tips, but the majority are FAR MORE interested in being entertained in one form or another!

Look at the success of the Geico insurance ads. They combine entertainment with a strong USP: SAVE MONEY ON YOUR AUTO INSURANCE! People love the commercials and their business has grown dramatically because they are entertaining and EFFECTIVE!

Make your marketing entertaining and you will increase the number of people who pay attention to it and the number of people who pass the message on to others!

But make sure the entertainment does NOT overshadow the REAL message.

CHAPTER 74

Outrageous Marketing Campaign Generates a Million Dollars in New Business for a Michigan Resort!

The first year Legendary Marketing had the Garland Resort account we produced the typical pretty, glossy resort brochure that ALL resorts have. Sure, compared to their previous brochure it had a lot more of the marketing elements that help drive response: better headlines, testimonials, benefit-laden copy, and calls to action. But still it looked and felt like a traditional resort-marketing piece.

The results were average so I proposed an audacious idea for Year Two. Ditch all their pretty marketing in favor of an outrageous, irreverent, and fun-filled magazine that resembled the *National Enquirer* rather than a four-diamond Michigan resort brochure!

CEO Barry Owens liked the audacity of the idea and was willing to take a leap of faith that the approach would cut through the clutter and deliver more business.

The 40-page *Garland Inquirer* was filled with shocking headlines, ludicrous stories, and funny pictures. Yet, despite all that, it managed to still sell the resort itself.

It's easy to get into a project like this and forget that while you want the piece to be entertaining the real test of success is to drive business. And drive business it did!

Garland mailed 100,000 magalogs (a magalog is a catalog that includes content — a magazine-catalog hybrid), 50,000 to their in-house list and 50,000 to various test lists. The response said Owens was "Just amazing. We had radio shows calling up, we were in the newspaper and on TV, and early copies changed hands on eBay for over $100!"

Middle Aged Brothers Claim 30 Years of Vacations at Garland the Secret to Their Amazing, Youthful Appearance!

Dan Parr, 42, pictured right, is younger than brother Peter, by almost a year, but few people can tell the difference. Says Pete, "It's amazing but we both still get carded at the Tiki bar. We started coming to Garland with our folks over thirty years ago. My dad taught us how to golf here, how to tie flys on the Au Sable River and we both learned to swim in Garland's pools. I had my first ever filet mignon in Hildegard's restaurant, rode my first horse and even met my wife here!

Yes, for us, Garland is so much a part of our lives we just couldn't imagine

going anywhere else on vacation. In fact now we own property here as well! I think it's the fresh air and pristine surroundings that helps relieve stress and keeps you feeling young.

Dan has his own ideas on staying young and is, in fact, in the process of writing a book about his philosophy entitled, "Garland – Your Secret Path to Never, Never Land!"

Inside sources have also confirmed he is in the process of negotiating a reportedly lucrative six figure deal from Oil of Olay!

Garland... Not Just Michigan's Most Beautiful Resort, But Michigan's Most Fun!

Here Are Dan's Ten Tips to Staying Young:

1. **You work hard, don't forget to take a break.** A weekend at Garland once a month will do wonders for your sanity!

2. **Commune with nature.** Hit the course or trails and enjoy the beauty of your surroundings while filling your lungs with good clean air.

3. **Take a spa treatment.** A good massage rids your body of aging antioxidants.

4. **Eat some fish.** The perch in Hildegard's is awesome and all those omega fish oils are great for your heart.

5. **Canoe the Au Sable.** The pristine scenery will free your mind and let your spirits soar. In fact, it may be the closest thing to heaven on earth.

6. **Get a good night's sleep.** Over the years my brother and I have stayed in just about every room on property and I'll tell you there ain't a bad room on the joint. That's important because you need a good cozy night's beauty sleep to stay young.

7. **Play one of the four magnificent golf courses.** Walk occasionally between shots. That will keep your heart rate up and burn enough calories for an extra beverage or two at the Tiki bar!

8. **Sing, laugh and dance.** All of which are scientifically proven to improve your health. With awesome entertainment by Jeff and Sue in the bar every night, it's an easy thing to do!

9. **Spend more time with family and friends.** If you hang around people you, like you, have more fun. Fun relieves stress and improves longevity. There is no better place to have fun in all of Michigan than Garland Resort!

10. **Sure you can't do the 100 yard dash in 11 seconds anymore but what the heck.** You can still sink the occasional 20 footer, out-drive your buddies once in a while and make the odd birdie here and there. Remember you are as young as you think you are. Focus on the positive!

If you'd like to stay young, take Dan's advice and call Garland! 1-877-853-3596. The sooner you call, the sooner you'll enjoy all the great anti-aging results!

Legendary Marketing used a unique blend of humor and benefit-laden copy to generate a massive response from the Garland Inquirer "magalog."

Snowmobiler's Flock to Garland After BIGFOOT SIGHTING in Lewiston

EXCLUSIVE STORY!

Lewiston, MI – Garland Resort already one of the world's most popular destinations for avid snowmobilers' with hundreds of miles of DNR trail right on its' doorstep is bracing for an influx of rabid riders after the seasons first Bigfoot sighting. First spotted just a few hundred years from Garland luxurious main lodge, three separate riders caught a glimpse of the elusive ape yesterday. Says Flint resident, Bob Ford, "I always love going to Garland to ride the trails but a Bigfoot sighting really adds to the excitement. We were so into it Saturday that we didn't even make it back to bar until 10pm, although in fairness we made up for our late arrival!"

If you want to join the excitement you can bring your own machine with secure onsite parking provided or you can rent one from Garland. Garland has hundreds of miles of groomed state and county wilderness trails, ranked among the finest in Michigan.

After an exhilarating day on the trails, guests here relax in style with hearty pub food or gourmet dining. Excellent nightly entertainment is provided and the cozy and luxurious accommodations will make you think your in a five star city hotel not lodged in the Michigan woods. Yet all ambience and luxury is delivered at surprisingly great winter values, although given the media hype it's advisable to book early.

Yet even with all the celebrities and news media floating around the grounds not everyone it seems, is here for Bigfoot. Sam Jones, of Lansing, said he was far more interested in the BIG JUICY steaks at Garland's Hildegard's restaurant than in some stupid ape! Either way if you're a Bigfoot fan or just a fan of a cozy winter escape with some of the world's best snowmobile trails on your door step make your tracks to Garland this winter. Even if you don't spot Bigfoot you'll have a great time trying!

Call 866-767-9721 Now To Book Your Next Exciting Snowmobile Excursion Or Ask About Our Garland Gift Certificates Today.

Garland...Not Just Michigan's Most Beautiful Resort, but Michigan's Most Fun!

Garland...Not Just Michigan's Most Beautiful Resort, but Michigan's Most Fun!

The follow-up winter version drew an equally favorable response.

Not Everyone Saw The Fun in It!

As expected, the response was not all positive. Owens laughs as he tells the story of a Garland property owner who called in shortly after receiving a copy of the *Inquirer*. Says Owens, "She told me she thought it was cheesy, classless, and not at all what she thought Garland was or should be doing. I asked if she disliked one article in particular? She said, no, she had read all 40 pages and hated them all! I mean, think about it — what's the chance that most people even read two or three pages of your typical brochure? People were actually sitting down and reading all 40 pages of the *Inquirer*. They were also calling up and requesting additional copies, or asking that we mail copies to their friends. It was just amazing!"

While Garland Resort expected to get a few negative calls, I also expected that, thanks to free pass-along and word of mouth, about 250,000 people we didn't send it to had read all or some of the magazine! Now that's what I call Cunningly Clever Marketing!

Here is the funny thing though — despite the *Inquirer's* over-whelming success, and despite the fact that Garland is a high-end property, I have showed the concept to other resorts, told them the staggering amount of money it generated, and they just shake their heads and say, "It's just not for us, Andrew!"

With the success of the summer publication we went to work on a winter edition complete with a Bigfoot story that, believe it or not, attracted a call from a man who goes around the world looking for Bigfoot. He was certainly disappointed when we told him the sighting was fake!

Download complete copies of the *Garland Inquirer* at:

www,CunninglyCleverMarketing.com

Why Did the *Inquirer* Succeed in Driving Garland's Business with this Approach?

The key is that Garland dared to be different. Garland has always set itself apart as a place to have fun. We wanted to carry that FUN aspect though into their marketing and let people know that Garland wants to provide them with a great time — before they come, while there, and even after they leave the resort!

So, how would you go about getting 100,000 people on your sales team? Do something outrageously fun with your marketing — something other customers and prospects can't wait to show their friends!

CHAPTER 75

Informational Magazine Drives Product Sales While It Entertains

Magazines don't have to be funny to be entertaining — they can also be informational.

When world-famous golf instructor David Leadbetter came out with a new training-aid product, the price of airtime for info-mercials had gone up so much that he had to look for other av-

Inform and sell!

enues to try to beat the 300,000 sales of his previous product. David has a large archive of great instructional books and materials. I suggested we use that as the basis for a golf tips magazine built around using the training aid to improve your game.

The magazine (or "magalog") we produced combined solid instruction fundamentals with picture sequences and drills featuring the training product. One hundred thousand copies were printed and mailed and visitors to the website could download the magazine as a pdf file. What makes this magalog format so effective is that it is essentially an infomercial on paper. It has all the same elements you would have on TV but is delivered on paper far more cost effectively.

Download a complete copy of the Leadbetter magazine at:

www.CunninglyCleverMarketing.com

The magalog strategy is an excellent idea for any product or service that needs a longer sales pitch to explain the product and build value.

CHAPTER 76

A Soft Sell with Big and Lasting Results!

Perhaps the most innovative giveaway we ever came up with at Martial Arts America was a coloring/activities book. They were 120 pages, cheap to produce, and lasted a long time. Not only did

we give the coloring books away to every single person who walked into our business with a young child, but we also had the coloring books out at restaurants as well as dentist, doctor, and chiropractic offices throughout town.

It was a tremendous source of new business because once a child started coloring in the book, he took it home. Once he took it home, he started to talk to mom or dad about wanting to do martial arts.

This free activity book was a Cunningly Clever way to reach kids.

And, when you turned to the back page, there was a beautiful full-color ad that talked about the many benefits of Martial Arts America for children.

Not to mention little Joe's constant reminders every time he opened the book. "Mommy, can I do karate? Can I? Mom, Johnny does karate; can I do karate?"

It really doesn't matter what business you are in, or even if children are your prime market. What matters is that they color in the pictures and show them again and again to everyone willing to look!

Entertaining children is a great way to reach parents!

CHAPTER 77

Building Your Client Base Early

Building a Future Client Base at Home Depot

In my area, Home Depot was giving FREE workshops to kids on Saturday mornings. My son made a model plane, a boat, a birdhouse, and a fire engine out of wood. While the kids were busy building, parents had an hour to kill wandering about the store.

Do you think they bought anything?

Talk about positive branding!? Every time I look at that bi-winged red plane, guess what company I think of? On top of that, where do you think these kids are going to tell their parents to shop? Where do you think these kids are going to shop when they grow up?

Barnes and Noble Offers Free Story Time

Saturday afternoons, my local Barnes and Noble bookstore offers children's story time. Just as with the Home Depot program, the parents linger in the store. They browse the aisles, drink expensive coffee, and buy into the brand in a bigger way than they otherwise would because now Barnes and Noble is not only entertaining their children, but they are encouraging the children to read and setting up their next generation of customers.

Show and Tell

In the karate business we had a very aggressive and sophisticated show-and-tell program for schools that I have also seen adopted by a local dentist, water conditioning company, and dog groomer. In fact, with a little creative variation, the technique could be used by almost any business. You simply tell all your young customers that when they have a show-and-tell day at school, you would like to participate. Our formally designed programs included excellent handouts that brought kids into the karate school in droves.

For complete details of how we ran our show-and-tells:

www.CunninglyCleverMarketing.com

How can your company reach and educate children in a positive way, which in turn would bring their parents to your business?

CHAPTER 78

Spreading the Good Word — Connecting with Customers After They Leave

I pitched this Cunningly Clever idea to two dozen partners over a two-year period before Garland Resort (ever my early adopter for anything out of the box) decided to try it, with spectacular results.

Upon check-out we gave each guest a free audiobook titled *Great Golf Storis for Your Drive Home* in a traditional CD jewel case. At the end of each story and at the beginning of each story — so you can't skip ahead — is an ad for some aspect of the resort: meetings, romantic getaways, special events, golf, winter sports, etc.

The guests, many of whom drive three hours or more from the Detroit area, now have a piece of Garland on their way home. They can be half way down I-75 yet still enjoying their Garland experience thanks to the audio CD!

Now, here's the best part. The next time they go golfing and have three others in the car (golfers often travel in fours), what CD do you think they put on? Right! — the golf stories CD.

When they get tired of it, what do you think they do? Throw it away? No, CDs have value ($15.95) so they are far more likely to give it to another friend who plays golf, expanding the reach once again.

www.GarlandUSA.com   1-877-4GARLAND
4700 North Red Oak Road, Lewiston, MI 49756

In the last four years Garland has given out more than 30,000 audios with an estimated listener base of over 200,000. "It's creative things like this that have helped us thrive in a very difficult economy!" says CEO Owens. Best of all, it's cheap, with CDs in volume costing under a buck!

To listen to the complete *Great Golf Stories* CD go to:

www.CunninglyCleverMarketing.com

This year Garland has ventured into rock music with a host of recognizable tunes modified and sung by their resident band Jeff and Sue. Songs include *Welcome to the Hotel Garland.*

A Fairway to Heaven, On the Course Again, A New Czar in Town, and ten other spoofs of popular songs.

To hear this awesome album of songs, go to

www.CunninglyCleverMarketing.com

I also combined audios with this marketing-through-kids concept back in the karate days, using stories for kids that contained the traits like persistence, confidence, and self-esteem that we were trying to teach. These served not only to take our message home to the parents paying the bills and therefore increased retention, but they also generated a ton of new business!

Audios have also been a leading part in my company's marketing for over two decades. I generate thousands of requests a year for my one-hour seminars like *The 12 Indisputable Laws of Marketing.* The CDs are informative, entertaining, and full of useful strategies anyone can use. But they are also a very strong sales pitch for my company and my services.

To listen to the *12 Laws of Golf Marketing,* go to:

www.CunninglyCleverMarketing.com

In some ways the CD is better than a phone pitch because prospects are most likely to listen to it uninterrupted in their cars. Often they will listen to it several times before calling us. This makes these prospects far more educated and therefore far more likely to buy. We generate a great deal of high-quality business from this strategy!

Audios are a great way to entertain and inform your customers while spreading your message to others who are just like them!

CHAPTER 79

Instructional DVD Entertains as It Sells

During a DVD shoot at Garland Resort we had some time left so I hooked up with the pro and we drove around the course shooting golf tips on Garland's best 18 holes. For an ad-lib production, it came out great and we decided to package it as *The 18 Greatest Golf Tips*. We used the DVD as a way to collect data, as a $19.95 value-added gift for golf groups, and as a thank-you gift to golfing guests.

Best of all, we sold a bunch of DVDs on the website for $4.95 to cover shipping and handling, which in fact covered all the costs!

We also managed to get a bunch of other courses to buy some DVDs at $2 to use as a value-added bonus for their guests, reducing distribution costs to zero and increasing our reach for nothing. Now that's Cunningly Clever!

A garden center can give landscaping tips; a health spa, beauty tips; a financial planner, retirement strategies. People are always hungry for information on topics that interest them!

To view a clip of the golf video go to:

www.CunninglyCleverMarketing.com

Giving instruction on DVD is a great way to provide valuable information and entertain your prospects while you sell them!

CHAPTER 80

Trump, Dr. Phil, Ozzey, Little Richard, Elvis, and Dr. Evil Lend a Marketing Hand

When the new season of Donald Trump's TV show *The Apprentice* was announced with the Celebrity Apprentice variation, we decided to jump on the bandwagon by producing a couple of viral videos timed to hit just as the show's publicity was in full swing. We found John Di Domenico, a tremendously talented actor who can don a variety of personas with amazing accuracy!

Our celebrity impersonator did a great job on our viral video.

We filmed a funny skit in the Garland boardroom and put it up on You Tube. With a couple of e-blasts to promote it we were able to notch up 20,000 views in a few weeks. Now this is not the type of marketing I'd personally want to spend a great deal of time doing, for while it's fun, it's very hard to measure results. That said, YouTube does offer some amazing opportunities to get the word out. For instance,

Top-Flite's *D2 Man,* a rap song, notched up over one million views in just a few months.

For optimal results, tie the viral component of your campaigns into the rest of your marketing as we did with the *Garland Inquirer,* rather than just doing one-of's!

View the videos at:

www.CunninglyCleverMarketing.com

Viral videos are cheap to make and if they are entertaining enough can build a huge following in a short period of time.

Just make sure the message gets through the fun!

CHAPTER 81

Why You Should Treat Your Customers Like Dogs

I am going to share with you a simple strategy to boost your image and popularity among all of your customers, create new opportunities with prospects, and massively increase your income — by treating your customers like dogs!

At least like my dogs!

Some years ago my dog, Winston, a black lab, needed a vet. My wife took him to the nearest local vet which at the time was Laguna Hills Animal Hospital. They took care of his problem and sent him home with some tablets.

A few months later, we moved some 30 miles away. Now, I'm sure you've had the same experience when you moved into a new home. You get truckloads of junk mail from Realtors, insurance agents, landscape contractors, pool services, and charities, all vying for a piece of your disposable income. However, I admit to being surprised when I found a letter addressed to Winston Wood.

I showed the envelope to my wife and commented that someone at somebody's headquarters must be really screwed up if they had started sending junk mail to dogs. Imagine trying to make a sales presentation to a dog!

However, when I opened the envelope on Winston's behalf, I discovered that it was no mistake. The contents were indeed intended for Winston Wood. Inside was a birthday card from the animal hospital. Immediately, I felt a guilty twinge because I had no idea it was his birthday. I jumped in the car and rushed down to the store to get him a bone. My wife and I laughed, put the card on a coffee table, and told all our friends about the incident.

My Dog Was Late on His 1040 Again This Year

Over the next few months Winston and my other dog, Sally, received several additional pieces of mail, all addressed to them personally. Believe it or not, Winston even received a 1040 DOG form at income tax time.

Although Winston loved to travel, Sally drooled and threw up every time she even saw a car. There were twenty veterinary clinics that were closer to our new home, all staffed with fine, caring doctors. Some may have been less expensive, and some of the nearby vets were my golf buddies. But where do you think I took my dogs when they needed care? Right again!

I drove 30 miles with Sally drooling all over my car and Winston hanging out the window, panting happily at other drivers. Why? Because I felt that if the vets took the time and effort to send cards to my dogs, they must be the best vets in town. People who care get my business, and these vets showed they cared by sending something tangible to me!

Their marketing was some the most Cunningly Clever, entertaining, and effective I have ever seen! The fact that I'm still talking about it more than a decade after I left California is one thing, and the number of people I showed the letter to while I was there was also astonishing, some of whom must have ended up as their customers!

People don't care how much you know until they know how much you care!

Form **1040-DOG**	**ALL Breeds**	Department of the Treasury — Internal Revenue Service U.S. Individual Income Tax Return	**2008**

Use IRS label	Registered Name:		Dog Tag Number: ◄
	Calling name:		
	Master's name:		Rabies ID Number: ◄

Filing Status
☐ Stray Dog   ☐ Family Dog   ☐ Top Dog   ☐ Underdog

Exemptions for Dependents
► Check all dependents: ☐ Fleas   ☐ Worms   ☐ Other dependents
☐ Ticks   ☐ Ear mites   ☐ All of the above

Income

1	Dry Kibble, and other gross income	1
2	Stolen roasts, turkeys, hams and other capital income	2
3	Income from beef by-products	3
4	Kidney, liver, and other organ meat	4
5	Compensation from hunting, herding, or watching	5
6	Show winnings	6
7	Acting fees (dog star)	7
8	Stud fees	8
9	Capital gains and appreciation of assets:	
a	Appreciation of personal assets	9a
► b	Appreciation of assets of other dogs	9b
c	Appreciation of doghouse	9c
d	Appreciation of buried bones not yet fully appreciated	9d

Credits and Deductions

10	Veterinary benefits:	
a	Credit for not trembling and wimpering in exam room	10a
b	Credit for not yelping during shots	10b
11	Casualty losses from accidental elimination (special allowance for puppies only)	11
12	Laundry expenses (ring around the collar)	12
13	Spay pay (credit for neutering)	13
14	Deduction for losses of tennis balls	14
15	Depreciation of rubber tug toy	15
16	Tax-exempt income from service as a guide dog for the blind	16
17	Damages from housebreaking	17
18	Poultry retrieval without appreciation	18
19	Impoundment charges	19
20	Fines for voluntary contributions to sidewalks and lawns	20
21	Credit for deposits behind bushes (safe deposit)	21
22	Interest in the deposits of others	22

Balance Due
Your total tax bite ►

Special Discount

Preparer's Use Only

Preparer: Laguna Hills Animal Hospital	Petland Veterinary Hospital
24271 El Toro Road Laguna Hills, California 92653 714 / 837-7333	23815 El Toro Road Ste. B El Toro, California 92630 714 / 581-0730
Firm's name (or yours if self-employed) and address ►	E.I. No. ►

Twenty years after my dog received his first one, this Cunningly Clever veterinarian still uses the 1040 PAW form to connect with customers.

9

Cunningly Clever
Offers

CHAPTER 82

Your Secret Weapon in the Battle for Massive Response!

I want to expose you to a truth, one that no one else in the advertising and marketing industry dares to tell you.

Ninety-nine percent of all your direct mail, print advertising, commercials, and Internet marketing is doomed to FAIL because of one KEY, missing ingredient — the lack of an irresistible offer!

A full 95% of the hundreds of sales letters I get and 99% of the thousands of ads, websites, and commercials I see each year fail in this most basic of all marketing principles, by simply failing to make any kind of attractive offer!

You can't make a mail campaign succeed with a BAD list. Nor can you make an ad campaign work with bad copy.

But the truth of the matter is, *you can* take an alarmingly average mailing list, ad, or website and still make a success of your campaign — **if you have an irresistible offer!**

Most do not.

An irresistible offer can often rescue an otherwise terrible marketing campaign!

CHAPTER 83

Why Understanding Lifetime Customer Value Is the Key to Unlocking Your Irresistible Offer

When I talk of irresistible offers at my seminars, the room goes quiet. It goes quiet because most people in business have a totally distorted view of what it takes to get a new customer, sale, or even a lead.

This makes them very reluctant to devise an IRRESISTIBLE OFFER, since they think that any OFFER would involve giving away or cheapening their product or service!

Very few of your competitors will ever answer the following questions or go through the simple but powerful exercise I suggest. This will give you a massive advantage because you will be working from FACTS, not vague guesses.

Do You Know What the Lifetime Value of Your Customer Is?

Do you know exactly how much it costs you to get a lead?

If you don't, there's no need to feel bad, almost no one does!

The math is simple. You just take your total marketing budget divided by your total number of leads generated per year. If you add in ALL of your marketing costs, newsletters, printing, parties, staffing, and so on, I can guess the number is almost certainly HIGHER than you thought it was!

If your referrals are taken out of the equation, it may be staggeringly higher than you thought!

Do you know exactly how much it costs you to make a sale? (Cost for leads divided by actual sales.)

Do you know what the lifetime value of your customers is? (The number of new customers times their yearly spending times the typical lifetime of a client, plus 4% a year inflation.)

What Is a Customer Worth to Your Business?

If you get a new customer to show up at your restaurant for a $50 meal, you gross $50. But if you get him back 10 times this year that customer is worth $500. Twenty times and he's worth $1,000! And that does not include whomever he brings with him, the occasional party, catering, and referrals.

That customer's true value might well be $2,000, for which you should gladly pay $100 or more to get him in the door.

Maximize Your Marketing Dollars

Now let's say we spend $12,000 on a direct-mail campaign to 10,000 restaurant goers in your area. What will the response be? I could tell you the typical response to a good list with good copy is 0.5%, but even that would be a stretch.

The truth of the matter is that all things being equal the amount of your response will be based on the quality of your offer!

You can get 1%, even 2%, or 3% response rates, BUT ONLY TO IRRESISTIBLE OFFERS. In fact, we have had response rates of 10%, 30%, 63%, and even more to well-executed campaigns.

- Offer a $5 discount to your restaurant...The response will be lukewarm at best!

- Offer a FREE bottle of wine and watch response SOAR!!!

- Tell people to come see your new homes in Florida because they are exclusive...yawn!

- Offer them two nights at the Ritz, a round of golf, and a property tour at a very attractive discounted rate and BOOM they are already on Southwest.com looking for a flight!

- Offer them $500 off the price of a new car, no big deal!

- Offer them a $2,000 trade-in on their old car as long as it has wheels...and ZOOM, they're down at your dealership!

Determine First What You Can Afford to Offer

In order to determine what value your optimum irresistible offer should be, you have to track your leads, conversions, and up-sells. It may well be okay to give away $60, $600, even $6,000 worth of gifts, bonuses, or incentives per person to attract new customers. Sure it might be a loss leader, although it certainly doesn't have to be. But even if it is, it's one that can pay off VERY QUICKLY in the form of ongoing business!!!

If you are willing to pay, say, $30,000 to sell a new home, instead of spending it all on marketing costs, get a viral campaign going. Spend $5,000 to tell people about the five years of FREE cruises, $15,000 in free furniture, or three-year lease on a new car that comes with your home, and put the other $10,000 in your pocket!

Please re-read this chapter; the concept is critical to your success. What would you pay to get a new customer right now?

Once you know what a customer is really worth, you can put a specific dollar value on creating your irresistible offer!

CHAPTER 84

WAIT! — My Product Is Wonderful and My Clients Are Sophisticated — I Don't Want to Offer Hokey Discounts and Special Offers!

When I start showing people some of the irresistible offers we have conjured up for our partners, they very often pull back and say something like:

> *Wait a minute. We are a high-end, sophisticated, old-fashioned (soon to be dead) business. Are you suggesting we offer these over-the-top types of promotions and discounts to our distinguished customers?*

Well, actually, YES!

What do you think are some of the key benefits for American Express Platinum or Black cardholders, the very elite of the spending scale?

DISCOUNTS, UPGRADES, and BONUSES!

Elite AMEX cardholders are offered discounts on cruises, free upgrades, free companion airline tickets in business class. Extra free room nights, $300 spa gifts, dinner with the ship's captain. Free limo pick-up to and from the airport, and a $3000 certificate towards the first month's private jet rental. And these are just some of the offers I got this month!

The fact is, I almost never get an offer from an American Express partner, ALL OF WHOM are at the PINNACLE of high-end, that does not offer a strong inducement to act now!

It's the same with the car rental companies, the cruise lines, catalogs, and the various high-end properties that want to sell me a quarter share of a second home. Even world-famous resorts like The Breakers, Pinehurst, and Pebble Beach send me offers that include large inducements, especially in their off seasons.

They all know that even at the higher end of the income scale, people are people. They want a deal. They want an offer. They want a special bonus, a justification for acting now, rather than next week, next month, or NEVER!

PLEASE MAKE NO MISTAKE ABOUT IT, the vast majority of the rich, the famous, the world travelers, are people just like you and me. They want to feel like they received a good value no matter what their income level. In fact, because they are successful professionals and entrepreneurs, very often they take more pride in getting a GOOD VALUE than the average Joe on the street.

People are people. They are vain, greedy, egotistical, fat, and looking for love the world over. Don't make the mistake of thinking your customers are any different!

CHAPTER 85

Offers Do NOT Have to Be DISCOUNTS!

Thinking is the hardest work there is, which is probably why people do so little of it!

—Henry Ford

A good offer can include an attractive price point, but it does not have to be a discount. In fact, very often a value-added offer will work better than a discount since many people reading your offer won't know what the regular price is anyway.

The key is to offer the highest value gift possible that you can get at the lowest possible cost.

That's why things like a free room upgrade, cabin upgrade, or class upgrade work well. These have a relatively high perceived value to the customer at almost no cost to the company. The same is true for adding a free extra night's stay, throwing in a second round of golf free, or offering an upgrade to a luxury car.

In any type of consulting business, adding a certificate for $500 for a free consultation is a proven winner. Information is also a low-cost, high-value way to "incentivize" professional sales. Three instructional DVDs and a manual might well have a value of $499 or more with an actual cost of just ten bucks; therefore they are a perfect giveaway to drive business! At my Marketing Boot Camps I have used truckloads of free information in order to drive attendance at the $1,595 event.

Waiving registration fees for clubs or associations is also a winner. In fact, in helping clubs and associations of all kinds sell memberships, one of the first things we typically do is to reinstate or raise the joining fee. In many cases, we do this just so we can give it away.

Not having a joining fee is nowhere near as good as giving the prospective member a $5,000 gift certificate to negate the joining fee — TRUST ME!

In selling cars or houses, giving away $5,000 in options or upgrades is a low-cost way to trigger a sale, especially at the higher end of the market where the aluminum shifter knob on a Porsche 911 Turbo is a $980 option that must cost all of five bucks!

Let me give you a recent example.

I was meeting with a developer who had just remodeled an old, downtown, waterfront hotel into condos. He sold out the units quickly but then the big credit crunch hit and 40% of the units fell out of escrow.

I asked him what he was willing to pay to sell a condo. He thought about it carefully and said $30,000. Since most of his buyers were young professionals in their late twenties or early thirties I had an idea. Most of these people had college debts, were just starting professional careers, or were recently married. They would have to choose between a home and other stuff like a new car.

What if they didn't have to?

What if they could buy a waterfront condo and get a FREE Corvette convertible? When I was in that age group I'd say "Sign me up!" The cost of a three-year lease on a Corvette would be way under $30,000 and the buyer could have his cake and eat it!

No justification to spouse, parents, or peers, just a FREE Corvette with the purchase of a very nice condo!

I had a friend trying to sell his Bentley on eBay at top dollar. With no sale after several weeks, I suggested he offer a free week at his beachfront mansion that he rented out sporadically at $10,000 a week. He changed the ad, threw in the $10,000 bonus that cost him nothing since the house was vacant more than half the time, and sold it in three days!

Look for powerful bonus incentives that cost less than you want to spend per sale but that have great sex appeal and high perceived value!

CHAPTER 86

Do Over-the-Top Offers Really Work?

Yes, far better than any other type of offer.

And what type of people do these offers attract?

Everyone from the CEO to the dishwasher — and all those in between.

Let me give you a scenario and you decide.

Say you and your 11 buddies take a golf trip every year in Northern Michigan. You have a choice of six or seven resorts that all meet your needs for accommodations and golf. They are, more or less, all priced about the same. Then, right out the blue, one of the resorts offers you over $1,500 in FREE gifts and prizes for your group to play.

All things being equal, where are you going to look first when it comes to picking this year's venue? The resort that meets your needs *and* offers you $1,500 of FREE gifts, of course.

A Tale of Two Offers

Let's compare the outcome of this $1,500-free-gifts campaign to a strikingly similar campaign the year before. That campaign offered each player an $80 tee gift as opposed to $1,500 in prizes.

Now the campaigns were not exactly apples to apples but they were close enough.

Tee gifts at $80 per player, for a group of 24 players, comes to $1,920 worth of free gifts per group. Yet, as successful as that offer was ($150,000 in revenue), it was 450% less effective in driving business than the next offer we made which was $1,500 worth of free gifts for your group ($684,000 in direct revenue)! Although the second offer actually gave less per player, it produced more than $500,000 in additional revenue over the prior offer!

Each of the last five years we have increased the value of the offer and each year business has gone up dramatically. This year the prize package was over $7,000 worth of gifts and produced $1.7 million in bookings with each package costing the resort less than $400!

The more amazing your offer, the more amazing your response.

PERIOD!

CHAPTER 87

Offer Terms to Enhance Your Irresistible Offer

One of the key ways I built my karate business and my website business quickly was the favorable entry and exit terms I offered potential clients, namely:

- no set-up fees

- no contracts

- cancellation at anytime

This was a risk in the karate business since the average student only stays three months. It was an even bigger risk in my web business as I needed to keep my clients more than nine months and sometimes more than a year just to get my set-up costs back. But with 96% retention my first few years in business, it was a bold move that soon paid off.

There is not much of an approval process for signing a contract you can get out of at anytime. And, the truth of the matter is, when a person wants out, holding his feet to the fire with a contract seldom ends up working anyway.

Payment Terms

If you look at the long-term value of a customer you will often find that offering generous payment terms will not only help you make more short-term sales but also more long-term income.

- Split payments over three years.

- Offer monthly rather than quarterly or yearly payments. (Do this only on automatic bank draft.)

- Consider factoring your contracts if you need short-term cash.

Simple contracts and easy payment options boost response!

CHAPTER 88

Reduce Risk and Build Trust to Make Your Offer Even MORE Irresistible

To increase response even further and reduce the perceived risk to your prospect, the final touch you can add to your irresistible offer is to give a guarantee. Make the prospect's act of choosing you a safe choice so that they can reap your benefits for themselves and their families.

The more risk you take away from the prospect and take on yourself, the more response you will generate. The more you reverse the risk in the prospect's favor, the greater your gains will be!

If there is even a hint of fear, loss, or indecision in the prospect's mind, the prospect will choose to procrastinate.

Offer a Money-Back Guarantee

If you have a legitimate business offer, which I am sure you do, the statistical chance of you having to refund money is low, very low. In over 20 years of offering money-back guarantees on my seminars, it has happened only once, and these are BIG-ticket events. It happened in the karate business 15 years ago, and that was because the guy showed up a day late for the event in Baton Rouge!

In selling millions of dollars in books, audios, and videos, refunds have been requested fewer than ten times in 20 years. And eight of those times, it was the delivery service losing the product more than once (Murphy's Law), usually with an overseas client, that caused the dissatisfaction, not the information or product itself.

Here are some examples of guarantees you might explore or modify to fit your needs:

- Try our service for 60 days; if after 60 days you find it's not for you, simply tell us and we will refund your fees no questions asked.

- Total satisfaction guaranteed — if any part of your meeting program is not what you had hoped, we will fix it at once or remove the item from your bill.

- Visit Opulent Heights and if you don't agree that it is everything we say it is in our brochure, we will refund your airfare up to $500!

Here is an example of a risk-reversal guarantee for one of my marketing seminars:

Triple Money-Back Guarantee!!

If you do not agree that the information we provide in the Legendary Marketing Boot Camp can instantly be used at your business to make at least an extra $50,000–$250,000 in income, I will:

1. Refund your entire $1,595 investment!

2. Allow you to keep all $3,000 worth of the bonus manuals and gifts!

3. And give you $100 in CASH out of my wallet for wasting your time!

If you can afford to turn down an offer like this, then you simply are not serious about wanting marketing success for your company! Take that one to the board and run it up the flagpole! You have nothing to lose and tens of thousands of dollars to gain.

Enroll now. Space is STRICTLY LIMITED to 30 people for this once-in-a-lifetime event that will prove to be the biggest bargain of your entire business career!

Reducing the prospect's risk increases business no matter what you are selling, what your price point, or what the rest of your offer happens to be!

CHAPTER 89

Ask for Specific Action on Your Offer

Ask for specific action from your reader in simple step-by-step language. The more specific your instructions are, the greater your response will be!

I use an interesting experiment at seminars where I ask everyone to stand up. The attendees all stand up. If I asked them to twirl around and do the hokey pokey, they would do that as well — for one simple reason — because I asked them to. They take action because they are asked to take action. If they are not asked to take action, they will sit there for hours on end just listening, waiting to be asked to do something. Sure, one or two in a hundred will ask questions of their own volition; the rest will wait until you tell them you want questions from the audience or signal that you require their participation in some other way!

Here are some examples of action-getting statements:

- Go to your computer right now and click on the "discover tour" icon located on the top right of the home page. Simply fill in a few brief questions and you'll be on your way to paradise...

- Call and book now; reservation agents are standing by to help you secure the best dates.

- Tell them:

    - Who to call by name

- When to call

- Add this number to your cell phone NOW; you never know when you might need it!

- When to stop in

- To book an appointment

- To go to your website now

- To check their calendar, then book

- To cut out your coupon and place it by the phone or on the fridge

- Be even more specific; cut out this coupon for a free tire right now and tape it to your steering wheel!

Put these calls to action at the bottom of every page of your website, on every page of your brochures, and in all your ads, emails and collateral materials — EVERY PAGE!

The more detailed your instructions for response, the greater the response!

CHAPTER 90

Quick, Quick, Hurry — Create a Sense of Urgency for Your Offer!

If you DO NOT ASK FOR SPECIFIC ACTION from your marketing, very few people will take it on their own accord. But asking for action is not enough; it's imperative that your offers also create a sense of urgency to ACT NOW!

Procrastination of any sort will destroy your response. You must get the reader to take action as quickly as possible and you must give him valid reasons for doing so NOW rather than keeping it in the "get around to it later" file. While some prospects will act later, the vast majority will not (the do-it-later file becomes the dead file).

Create a sense of urgency in one of the following ways...

Limit the amount you have to sell:

- Only 10 lots are left at this price!

- Only 18 Charter Memberships will ever be sold, each with all the additional privileges I have just described.

- Only five in stock, available for immediate delivery now!

- Only six prime meeting dates remain — book now!

- Only one red-and-tan car on the lot!

Limit the date by which they can buy at this price, or talk of an impending increase in prices:

- As soon as phase one is completed, prices will jump by $50,000 per unit; act now and gain instant equity over phase two!

- The marketing committee is currently discussing a substantial increase in prices to bring them more in line with other companies, none of whom offer the same level of quality, service, and flexible payments you will find at...

Talk of a limited number of bonus items to accompany your offer:

- We have only a limited supply of the items included in our $1,500 bonus package and can only accommodate the first 25 groups.

Talk of lost opportunity:

- Our last phase sold out in less than six months and enjoyed rapid appreciation; I urge you to act now.

- Those who book their cruises early get the best cabin choices and free upgrades.

- Only six of last year's model remain, and then the opportunity for substantial savings will be gone forever.

Talk of social, financial, and prestige gain:

- You have worked hard to get where you are. Now it's time to reward yourself with an automobile befitting your standing in the community.

- While obviously the motivation to join a top club like Legendary Country Club is more for personal enjoyment than business, many professionals are quietly amazed at the increase in business that seems to follow them joining the club.

Give them the whole kitchen sink and include every one of the previous examples in a super-charged offer backed by an ironclad guarantee! It is almost impossible to use too many techniques to elicit response!

Those who opt for the "understated" when it comes to creating a sense of urgency are simply deluding themselves into less sales!!!

CHAPTER 91

Test a Series of Different Offers to Tap into Different Motivations

While there is much to be said for repetition in any marketing effort, the words of W.C. Fields ring out loud and clear: "If at first you don't succeed, quit! There is no use being a damn fool about it."

All kidding aside, test your marketing. Especially when doing multiple mailings, you can vary the offer to match different motivational factors in the reader.

For example:

In the first four letters of our successful Thunderbolt campaign for a resort, we used $3,500 worth of prizes as the offer.

In letter five we switched the offer to a free romantic getaway with the wife, playing on the possible guilt, or the wife saying "What do *I* get out of it?" factor.

In letter six we opted for plain old bribery with $50 in resort cash per guest, redeemable anywhere on property.

Last, but not least, we offered to stop killing trees! A reference to all the letters we were sending them, and instead offered to plant a tree in their honor on the course.

One group, whose leader had just died, opted for the trees and brought in $28,000 in business. They all had a great time with the planting ceremony on the 18th hole. A brass plaque with the leader's name was placed on the tree, and they even sprinkled his ashes into the hole for good measure!

Each of these additional offers produced business we would not have gotten had we stuck with just one offer!

Which, naturally, brings us back to the importance of testing.

Test, Tweak, and Test Again

Testing offers is another area of marketing success that most people don't want to talk about. They don't want to talk about it because it costs money to test. Yet with the best efforts in the world you cannot maximize your marketing success without it.

The plain truth of the matter is that some offers just work better than others, and it's not always the ones you think will work that prove to be the most successful.

You must commit to testing various offers in order to maximize your response!

10

Maximizing Your Profits

CHAPTER 92

Hunting for Big Game!

Imagine for a moment that you are stranded in a mountain cabin by a freak snowstorm. You have been there a week when one morning the weather breaks, but it's obvious you won't be going anywhere for a while.

You are out of food and haven't eaten for a few days when you wander out onto the deck with the single-shot rifle you found in the cabin. Bingo, your luck has changed. Right in front of you is food! The food comes in several sizes: three rabbits, two coyotes and a moose — each just 10 feet from your nose.

You have never shot anything in your life but you have a choice to make and your life depends on it. You don't know how long it will be until you are rescued and you badly need a meal. Which animal do you try to shoot with your single-shot rifle?

I hope you said the moose because the moose will not only provide you with the biggest, easiest-to-hit target but also with the biggest payoff in terms of food. It's a pretty obvious example but at the same time it's the one least often applied in most business situations. As the great advertising guru David Ogilvy once said, "If you have to hunt for business you might as well hunt for good business!" Most business owners still go after rabbits rather than moose; they fish for minnows rather than whales. Yet 10,000 minnows do not equal one whale any more that 10 rabbits make a moose.

I often hear business owners complain about the type of clients they get in their doors. They are getting low-end, bottom feeders they complain. They don't spend enough or stay long enough. They opt for the cheapest product over quality, and so on. The funny thing is that when I ask them what type of marketing they are doing to attract new clients, it's usually mass-mailing discount coupons or discount-oriented print ads in the local paper.

Let me give you an example. My wife is in the market for a new truck and every car dealer in Citrus County ought to know that in a big way. Why?

Because she is just a couple of months short of the end of her lease on her existing vehicle. It's a high-end SUV and we live in a high-end neighborhood. What are the chances that she will keep the SUV for another year once the lease runs out? Almost zero — in fact, we are already overdue for a new car.

Some car dealer in Citrus County should know that. They should know that because of the lease dates, the registration, or by whatever means they use, but they should know that. The dealer I bought my last car from should certainly know that. They should have called. They should have asked if they could drive around to my house and let my wife test drive the latest model of the same vehicle. On a $60,000 SUV, you should get personal attention.

Instead of spending a little time going after people who have already demonstrated that they have the desire and money to own such a vehicle, they run full-page ads and send out John Doe letters fishing for unqualified minnows.

A daily-fee golf course spends $600 for a discount ad in the local paper to attract individual players at a marginal rate. Instead, they should occasionally break the mold by taking the $600 and using it to send 1,200 sales letters to all the local charitable, fraternal, and fund-raising organizations. The letter would advertise their tournament and event services. If just one organization out of 1,200 books an event, they might get 144 players to show up. If 1% of the 1,200 people who get the letter book an event, that would be 12 events, or well over 1,000 players. Compare that with 30–40 people who clip the discount coupon to save $20! The difference is staggering, but most businesses just don't do it.

Instead of spending $600 on an ad or a mailing, how about hiring a temp for the week and spending the $600 calling all the people who bought a car from you three years ago this month, held a golf tournament last year, or donated to your charity. If they make 50 contacts per day, that will be 250 in a week and that's low. What could your business accomplish if you called 250 of your best customers? Could you resell them or up-sell them? Of course you could and that's my whole point!

Hunt for big game first and the small fry will take care of themselves.

CHAPTER 93

Cruising on the SS Income Maximization

I recently enjoyed a very pleasant cruise with my family in the Baltic. All the cruise lines are masters of the add-on, the up-sell, and the re-sell. All use aggressive direct mail, value-added bonus gifts, and loyalty programs. In fact, one of the main reasons for the massive growth of the cruise industry over the last decade is the fact that they have outmarketed many of the other vacation options.

What really impresses me is not the ships, the food, or the service, but the tireless way in which they develop and market their multiple streams of revenue! Of course the cruise lines have the added advantage of a truly captive audience, but there is much that all businesses could learn from the cruise industry.

They are industrious and focused in their efforts to get their passengers to part with the maximum amount of money in the shortest possible time! While, of course, providing them with a good time.

There are up-sells for the ship's tours at each port of call. All with very impressive markups over what you can do on your own. (In many cases hiring a private car, driver, and guide were cheaper than putting my family of four on the tour bus!)

While most food is included on board, you can, for a small fee, usually twenty dollars a head, upgrade to a special dining room. Which was always busy, despite, as far as I could tell, serving the same menu anyway!

Either way, you pay — and pay well — for wine and wine packages at dinner. Buy five bottles for X, seven for Y and the choice selection of 10 for Z!

Drinks are an up-sell 24/7 and, of course, there is always a daily drinks special.

They offer onboard gambling, shopping, and lectures.

They offer Internet access for an exorbitant fee, DVD rentals, and, on some ships, jet ski, kayak, or boat rentals.

Then you can buy photos of you and your family getting on the boat and pictures getting off the boat with whatever cartoon character happens to represent the port. There are pictures at formal night, pictures at casual night — in fact pictures about every other bite at dinner! Pictures that are on display and for sale within minutes of the first click of the camera lens. All very efficient, and no doubt very profitable, if not somewhat annoying after you buy the first lot!

Many of the lectures, like those on wine, diamonds, or fine art involve — surprise, surprise — selling some of the above. Each day they have a different market (tables selling goods of the day depending on what port you are in).

The spa has daily specials and, while some of the fitness activities are free, you can, of course, sign up for yoga, Pilates, or whatever the exercise craze of the week happens to be at an extra charge.

They up-sell you on future cruises with special gifts if you book on board.

Few businesses do as good a job maximizing their income as the top cruise lines! In port in Estonia — well worth a visit!

Even during the disembarking seminar they tell you it's hard to get a cab dockside (hard to believe) and that you can take their bus to the airport, station, or town for a small extra fee!

Yes, ladies and gentlemen, the cruise lines are the masters of customer maximization!

First, they identify every possible way of increasing incremental income.

Second, I am sure they set goals for each income possibility or discontinue the activity.

Third, they market each option aggressively with daily announcements, newsletters, and flyers.

In my case, the add-ons — without taking a single ship-sponsored tour — were 25% of the price of the cruise. But compared to most people I talked with, this was low. If you took even three or four of the tours, you were at 50% and if you took them all you could easily reach an additional 100% of the cruise's cost.

Now imagine for a moment that you could take each of your

existing members, customers, clients, partners — whatever you like to call them — and increase the revenue you generate from them by 25%, 50%, or even 100%! It sounds impossible, but it's not. In fact, 25–30% is very do-able; it's just that most businesses can't see the forest for the trees!

There is a fine line between increasing income in multiple streams and nickel-and-diming a valuable buyer to death. This is a line the cruise lines arguably cross but get away with because the people are captive. With a little thought and some trial and error, a reasonable balance can be achieved that results in additional services for your customers and additional income for you!

Maximize income from your existing customers before chasing new customers.
It's often possible to double or even triple your profits without a single new client!

CHAPTER 94

Black Belts, Blizzards, and Sunscreen! The Critical Importance of Perfect Timing

One critical marketing factor that's not given enough attention is timing. For example, January is the best month to generate response by direct mail. It's 50% more effective than the next best month and hundreds of percentage points more effective than August, the worst month!

Despite this fact, billions are spent mailing offers in nonproductive months!

In the karate business, advertising in July and August was a complete waste so I stopped doing anything in those two months. Instead I doubled up spending in September when the kids went back to school and the parents were back in a sign-up mood — with impressive results.

In the golf business, the majority of clubs do their next year's budgets in October and November, hence they are our two most productive months for leads and sales.

When selling long-term programs in the karate business, selling upgrades six weeks after the student signed up and just after they passed their first test when their excitement was at its peak was staggeringly more profitable than pitching them two weeks earlier or later!

Sending e-marketing for Florida hotels right after the first big snowstorm up north produces astonishingly better results than if the weather was normal winter weather, so we always have a blizzard special loaded in and waiting for the right day to send it!

Health clubs and weight-loss centers sign up more people in January than any other month because people are in a New Year's resolution mindset! It rarely lasts until February!

Put sunscreen at the check-out counter when the weather is hot!

Every business has cycles for leads, sales, and upgrades. Some are obvious, many are not. Knowing exactly what yours are and focusing your marketing in these times, at the exclusion of all other times, will increase your success dramatically at no extra cost!

CHAPTER 95

Cashing In on Your Hidden Assets

Very often when I do an initial marketing audit for a company, I find the company is sitting on a gold mine of opportunity and cash without even knowing it. Other times the opportunity does not arise until they need money or incentives but the opportunity is always there!

One partner was looking for a number of incentives to increase the value of the packages they offered; however, while they wanted to offer several thousand dollars worth of incentives to their customers, they didn't want to spend more than $600 per incentive package.

First, I pointed out that they were getting 25,000–30,000 unique web visitors per month. There had to be a number of people who would like to capitalize on this targeted traffic.

Second, I noted that they had over 50,000 people on their email list, something many people would gladly trade for.

Third, their postal list of customers offered a way to make cash while their unused inventory of rounds and rooms was potential money in the bank.

In less than three months we had leveraged almost $600,000 worth of products and services without spending a dime in cash.

We used the products to sweeten our package deals and

doubled — yes, doubled and eventually almost tripled — sales from $600,000 to $1.3 million to $1.7 million, spending less than twenty grand on marketing!

Every company has hidden assets that cost them nothing but are of great value to others. What are yours?!

CHAPTER 96

Customer Audit Reveals Hidden Gold

Performing a customer "audit" can be one of the smartest things a business can do to uncover massive new business opportunities.

I first did this by accident twenty years ago trying to help a karate school owner increase his student base. As we talked I asked him to bring out his student list and go through it one by one. I asked who they were and what he knew about each: where they worked, what they did, who they might know, and whatever else he could tell me about them.

As it turns out, it was a small community and he knew a great deal about most of them. After about an hour we came to a man who worked at the Tyson chicken plant, by far the largest employer in the area. He worked in human resources and a short time later we approached him with the idea of a corporate karate program. Twenty-two people signed up, which was the equivalent of three or four months' sales in one day!

I went back and did the same thing with my own clients, going over each client with my staff. It turned out three of them were executives of major associations. Within three months and with a little incentive, those three customers alone brought us more than $150,000 worth of residual business! Had we not done a customer audit they may have continued on as three individual customers, just as they had for months before, producing $750 a month instead of $150,000!

At a new real estate development we found a Filipino couple who had bought a lot. The couple had a large extended family and we approached them with the suggestion that the development would be a great place for their family and friends. They accounted for eighteen lot sales that year!

Every business has customers of unusual influence in their community or industry. Their network of influence should be uncovered and mined to your mutual advantage!

CHAPTER 97

Powerful Strategic Alliances

By forming the right strategic alliances, a small business can become a big business overnight. An unknown person can become well known on the back of someone more famous and distribution costs can be cut while profits rise. There is, as they say, strength in numbers — in this case the sharing of resources, knowledge, and ideas.

Few wars are ever fought without such alliances and, in the corporate world, few large companies try to go it alone. They recognized a long time ago the value of strategic alliances to drive customers to each other. Automakers recommend specific car-care products in the owner's manual, earning themselves a residual payback in the process. Restaurants align themselves with soft drink companies, limo services, and credit card companies. In all its literature, Delta Airlines suggests that I sleep in a Hilton hotel and recommends that I rent my car from Avis. Even milk carton manufacturers team up with nonprofit agencies to look for missing kids.

Driving traffic to your doors with strategic alliances is not just relevant for big business. Nightclubs and restaurants often form strategic alliances with cab drivers to bring business right to their doors. A local hair salon was one of my best sources of leads for my first karate school. An alliance with a well-liked bartender can be a wonderful source of leads for just about every business in town.

Start with your friends and see what you can do for each other. How about giving out coupons for each other on your counters? Who do you know that has a list of customers and could write them a letter endorsing you? When you've practiced with friends, approach logical business partners you don't know. Helping each other get business is a nice way to get acquainted!

Who can you form a strategic alliance with to drive business to your doors?

CHAPTER 98

Getting Your Message to the Perfect Target Market — for FREE!

Perhaps the greatest benefit of forming a strategic alliance is the massive dent you can make in your distribution or marketing costs while increasing your reach.

Irvine Dance Academy had 1,200 little girls as their students, a vast majority of whom also had brothers. Their parents were already well tuned into spending money on after-school activities to enhance their children's lives. I steered potential dance students to Irvine; Irvine steered potential karate students to me.

Macho martial arts products was one of the two national companies that supplied martial arts schools with uniforms and equipment. They were in frequent phone and mail contact with every school owner in the country. I formed a strategic alliance with them and they distributed my sales literature to all of their clients for free. In return I promoted their products and included their logo as a sponsor on events I ran in the industry.

I had the same type of arrangement with Markel Insurance who mailed information on my seminars to over 10,000 karate schools in return for sponsorship of the events and a free booth at my annual trade show. Just the distribution of sales information alone to their customer base of karate business owners saved me thousands of dollars a year in postage.

As an added benefit I was also able to gain stature and visibility by in effect having these larger, more-established companies endorse my products. You can do the same in your business — no matter what it happens to be.

Garland Resort has over 50,000 active Michigan golfers on their mailing and email lists. When the snow starts, these customers don't play much golf. Meanwhile down in Florida the weather is perfect at Innisbrook resort and the smart-thinking people there are more than happy to provide Garland with a bunch of free vacations for access to that list! We mention Innisbrook in our Garland e-blasts and on their website while we pick up a bunch of free Florida vacations we use to attract group business to Garland!

My company made a similar deal with Club Profit Systems which sells point-of-sale solutions to over 900 golf clubs. I want to sell the same people website solutions. We cross promote each other with sales letters endorsing each other's products. There are few strategies more effective than this one!

Making alliances with companies whose customer profiles are very similar to yours to distribute each other's messages is one of the most effective and profitable marketing strategies you will ever find.

CHAPTER 99

Building a Referral Machine

Ask any good business how they generate most of their sales and they will instantly and enthusiastically tell you they do it through referrals. However, if you ask them to explain their referral system to you, you are very likely to get a blank stare or a shrug.

Only this week I asked the vice president of a major real-estate developer, the owner of large law firm, and the CEO of a major service company what type of referral system they had in place. All had the same answer — they didn't. Referrals just happen. So does death, but it doesn't mean you should wait around for it!

Referrals are the lifeblood of any good business. There is simply no quicker and less expensive way to build your customer base and increase your income than to double or triple your referral rate. It doesn't matter what type of business you are in, referral business makes you more money than any other type of new business. Referrals cost little or nothing to get and they come with the healthy endorsement of a friend or neighbor.

While some referrals will happen by accident, you cannot build a reliable marketing system on accidents. You have to plan, measure, and implement a referral system that insures two or three referrals from every single person with whom you come into contact.

The age-old business adage that what gets measured gets done is just as true for referrals as for any other part of your business. Referrals are a far too important part of your marketing strategy to leave to mere chance as most do. If you track sales calls, closing ratios, and up-sells, you should track referral generation as well — it's a great indicator of future business prospects!

Referrals must be sought from every customer, every client, every contact, and every supplier that does business with you. Furthermore, they must be sought out from all your personal relationships, from your accountant to your dry cleaner! Ask everyone!

The only way you can see whether your referral program is working is to set referral goals for your staff and measure your progress against them monthly!

CHAPTER 100

Understanding the
Psychology of Referrals

Start building your referral machine by first looking at the psychology of referrals. Many people are reluctant or embarrassed to ask for referrals. They fear people will think them pushy, a failure, or — worse still — reject them! Nothing could be further from the truth. People actually LOVE to give referrals — you just have to ask!

Giving referrals involves two contrary impulses. First, people like to give referrals because it allows them to help others at low cost to themselves. It makes them feel good about themselves and be a "hero" to others. Second, people worry about giving referrals because if something goes wrong they get the blame. And if things go right, the thanks they get is usually small. Because of this ambivalence, it's easy to get some people to give referrals and hard to get others to. Even the same people may change their attitudes over time. Clearly, your job is to encourage referrals and also make it *safe* to give referrals to your business.

People like to give referrals for three important reasons:

The first is ego. When someone buys a new home, car, or investment, he wants his friends and neighbors to be impressed. He wants them to know what a great deal he got. When was the last time you met someone who bought a new car and told you what a schmuck they were for buying it? It simply doesn't happen

— at least not in the first few weeks!

The second reason is that most people like to feel important; they like to be the center of attention or information. When the opportunity to take center stage arises by giving a referral, they are more than ready to step up to the plate.

The third reason is that birds of a feather flock together. People like their friends and neighbors to share and experience the same things they do! There are two parts to this equation. The first is the obvious that people want their friends to share in the joy of the same experience. The second and less talked about is that people want their friends to share the risk. If they are going to spend big money to join the country club then they want a friend to do it as well. Then if it turns out not to have been such a great idea, at least they are in it together. Few people talk about this side but it exists nonetheless — the "I'll do it if you'll do it" syndrome!

Never ask, "Do you know anyone who might _____?" Instead ask, "Who do you know?" The first approach generally produces an immediate "Oh, I'll have to think about it," while the second approach actually gets them to think about it! It's a subtle but huge difference!

People LOVE to give referrals. Make it easy for them by reminding them that you are looking for and want good referrals!

CHAPTER 101

How to Ask for Referrals So You Get Them from Every Single Customer Without Fail!

Imagine tripling your referral rate by simply demanding that your customers provide them? Sounds a bit unlikely, I know, but it's actually not that far-fetched at all.

In the karate business, many schools adopted a policy that in order to become part of the school's "Black Belt Club" (the ultimate up-sell), you had to introduce two new students to the school. It was written right into the sign-up contract as a condition!

I frequently write such conditions into my speaking contracts. Sometimes I do it as a bonus based on a Legendary performance, in other cases I do it as part of my up-front fee. My fee is $15,000, or $10,000 plus two personal introductions to someone else who has the means to book me.

Or, if the referrals are bonus-based, the contract might read, "$12,000 and, provided you are happy with my performance, you provide either a $3,000 bonus fee or two direct contacts within your industry."

Often they forget about the bonus after the event — but you'd be surprised how quickly they come up with two referrals when faced with that simple task or the $3,000 invoice on their desk and a copy of the signed contract spelling out the deal!

In my speaking surveys of audience members, I always request ONE referral to another group they know who could benefit from my program. Most people, because it's a specific request, fill it in!

There are more subtle, but equally effective, techniques than demanding referrals. When we sign up a new member at one of my country club partners, we immediately invite the new member to bring three guests.

"Dr. Smith, welcome to the club. As a way of thanking you for joining and, as our way of introducing the club to your friends, we have three complimentary green-fee certificates for you. We'd like to schedule your first tee-time for you and three friends. I need to fill in the names before I give them to you — whose name should I put on this first one?"

They ALWAYS come up with three names! This is another example of something I adopted from my years in the karate business. When little Johnny would sign up for lessons, we'd say something like this to his mother:

> "You know, Mrs. Jones, when a student comes in for his first lesson, often he feels a little out of place with everything that's going on until he gets to meet some of the other kids. I'm going to assign one of my best students to look after Johnny but if Johnny wants to bring a couple of friends in, that would be fine also. With that, I'd pick up two guest passes and look at Johnny, "Johnny, whose name shall I write on these guest passes?"

Set the expectation up front with your customers that if you deliver great products and services as promised, you expect, or even demand, their referrals!

CHAPTER 102

Be Specific When Asking for Referrals

Once you receive a referral, make every effort to get a little background on the person you will be dealing with. When I was selling my consulting services for karate schools a few years ago, I asked each client to provide me with three referrals. One client in Mississippi faxed me right back with the names of three people.

The first sneered when I mentioned who our mutual friend was, but was none-the-less mildly interested.

The second told me that if this particular client was using me then he certainly wouldn't.

The third started shouting at me on the phone at the mere mention of his name, and went on to tell me what he would do with the "son of a bitch" if he ever got hold of him.

I was completely confused and called the client back to ask him what was going on. He said he had simply referred people to me who he knew needed my services. He didn't know they had to like him!

Whenever you get a referral, try to find the REAL connection between the person referring and the referree. Ask how Joe knows Harry. Ask how long Sally has been friends with Chelsea. Ask what line of work the prospect is in. The more information you have about the referral and the clearer you are about the referrer's relationship with the referree, the better are your chances of a successful presentation.

When you get a referral, also use the referrer as a source of information about what the referree needs. Then find out something about the relationship between them!

CHAPTER 103

Diamonds under Your Feet — Opportunity Is Everywhere — You Just Have to Look

For years I have been going down to Moroso Motor Sport Park in West Palm Beach to race my car at the Ferrari Club's annual Maranello Madness event. To get to the track you have to drive right past the front door of PGA National Resort and then 8 miles into the boonies. In other words, PGA National would be

Maranello Madness every November should be a huge opportunity for the closest hotel.

an ideal location for us to stay, yet in a decade it has never been the club's host hotel.

Every car club in the world — Corvette, Porsche, Aston Martin, Viper, Lamborghini, etc. — all rent the same track at least once a year and very often twice. Every one of them has to drive past PGA National to get there. Almost all the events are two-day events. Almost all have a banquet and a concourse where people polish their cars and display them on the lawn. (Not me!) All surely have the income and general travel habits to be PRIME resort clients. Best of all from the resort's perspective, at least 80% of the events are off season and they often draw people from out of state who come in the night before, generating an extra room night. To top it all off, at least 10% of the participants will statistically be golfers!

When I mentioned car clubs as a prime prospect to the good people in the previous management at PGA National, they had simply never considered it! Although they thought it sounded like a good idea!!! (New Management: Take NOTE!)

Because of their unique location, they should have had a direct-mail campaign aimed at the decision maker of every major car club in Southern Florida.

Very often the most obvious prospects for your business, the ones right under your nose, are the ones you miss, so TAKE ANOTHER LOOK AROUND YOU!

ifi

Personal

Marketing

CHAPTER 104

So What Do You Do for a Living?

You are at a party and someone asks you a simple question the answer to which may have a huge impact to your personal success. It's a question you've been asked a thousand times and most likely answered without much thought.

"What do you do for a living?"

Now you may think this is a really easy question to answer, especially if you've been in business for a number of years. But at seminars you'd be amazed at the different responses I get to that simple question, even from a group of people all in the same profession such as accountants, car dealers, or Realtors.

A Saturn dealer and a Rolls Royce dealer may both sell cars but they are hardly in the same business. A Saturn dealer sells transportation; a Rolls dealer sells luxury.

A Timex dealer sells watches; a Rolex dealer sells jewelry.

Let's take Realtors as a simple everyday example. When I ask what business they are in at a seminar, I typically get these responses.

- I'm a Realtor, I sell homes.

- I'm in the service business.

- I'm in the people business.

- I'm a relocation specialist.

If you met these four people casually at a party, based on those statements who would you use?

Well, that might depend on what you wanted to do. If you wanted to relocate, you would most certainly choose the relocation specialist. Even though all the others may have offered this service, only one positioned himself as an expert on the issue.

However, you might not have picked him had you just wanted to sell your home.

If a fifth Realtor entered the picture with a statement that she was in the business of maximizing profits for people with real estate to sell, it would be a no-brainer. You would select her at once. Her message is focused, it's specific, and it's exactly what you and everyone else looking to sell a house needs — a maximum return on their real-estate investments.

All things being equal, three of the other Realtors lose out because of their positioning statements. Saying that you are in the service business is nebulous, the people business is nebulous, and selling homes is obvious, leaving only two answers out of five that actually offer some kind of competitive advantage in the marketplace.

You might argue that a specific positioning statement limits your market, but that, my friends, is the very idea. You limit your market to the one thing you can do best. This gives you an advantage. Then you harp on it for all you are worth and develop your own niche market within a much broader category.

The question "What do you do?" should be answered memorably in 10 seconds or less, positioning you in the right place for future business no matter what your product or service happens to be.

CHAPTER 105

Would You Buy a $200 Pair of Jeans from Bruce Lipshitz?

Company names can make or break a business. For your personal branding, your name can make a huge difference when it comes to building your reputation and image in the marketplace.

Would Tiger Woods be so appealing if everyone was calling him by his given name of Elderick?

Some names just don't conjure up images of success and high status.

Why do movie stars and pop stars change their names?

Because Norma Jean sounds common, but Marilyn Monroe sounds alluring.

Because Marion Morrison doesn't quite sound as tough as John Wayne.

Because Elvis Costello sounds a lot more intriguing than Patrick Mcmanis.

The answer is, your name projects your image!

Would you pay a real premium to wear Lipshitz suits or jeans? Probably not, but for Calvin Klein you might!

Alphonso D'Abruzzo was having a lot of trouble getting an acting job. But when he changed his name to Alan Alda, he became a TV legend playing "Hawkeye," another great name, in the long-running TV series MASH.

People associate certain names with trust and leadership. Names like John, Jack, and Tom are good solid names that generally elicit a positive perception. People associate other names with slyness, whimpiness, or trickery. Slick Willie, Tricky Dicky, and other such nicknames are common in English-speaking countries.

Comedian Rodney Dangerfield had a classic comedy routine where he said, "If I ever get in a bar fight I'm going to stop and check out where the guy's from. If he's from Sparta or Troy I'm outta there. What I really hope is that the guy's from Pleasantville, (New Jersey). After all, how tough can someone from Pleasantville be?"

I use my middle name as my professional last name rather than my given last name because it just sounds better! Others use a nickname or initials to increase their visibility and build their reputations. Check out your name and look at the perceptions it might create in the minds of a customer or client. If those perceptions are not good, consider a change. It's really not that hard!

In fact, thousands of corporations a year change their names, and the individuals who do so number in the tens of thousands. For a list of famous people and their real names visit:

www.CunninglyCleverMarketing.com

Perceptions are hard to change, names are easy.

CHAPTER 106

Bag Boy Doubles His Profits with a Cunningly Clever Change in Job Titles

With a little ingenuity you can turn the most mundane-sounding job or business into something that sounds exciting, more prestigious, or at least encourages questions that open up greater possibilities.

My very first job was as a bag boy at the Wellington Country Club in West Palm Beach, Florida. My typical work was to sit outside on the wooden bag rack, baking in the sun, waiting for the big old cars to roll to a stop. Then leaping into action, I pulled their giant, oversized golf bags out of their trunks and expertly secured them to a golf cart not ten yards away.

I never much cared for the title "bag boy" and one day, more for a joke than anything else, when someone asked me what my position at the club was, I told them I was "Director of Bag Operations." They seemed to buy the idea with no comment, and shortly after that I had a small number of business cards printed up with my name and that title.

Within a few weeks, an amazing thing happened, people started to treat me with a little more respect, and my tips (profits) actually doubled!

You can change people's perceptions of you, your product, or your service, and increase the amount they are willing to pay, with a small shift in positioning how you present yourself.

CHAPTER 107

How You Can Become the World's Leading Expert in Your Industry in Less than 60 Seconds!

In 1989 I had been in the karate business for just over two years as a full-time school owner and as a part-time instructor and hanger-on almost four. I had just come off my best year ever, having mad $120,000 from my 1,250-square-foot location.

At the time I was oblivious to what anyone in the industry beyond my small circle of local schools was doing. All I knew was that I was making two or three times what they were. I didn't know there were huge schools on the East Coast, billing companies that offered advice, and numerous large and powerful sanctioning organizations. All I knew was that I was more financially successful at running a martial arts school than anyone I had ever met, so I decided to write a book about how to run a successful school.

A year later when I finally published it as a manual in a three-ring binder, I billed myself as the world's leading expert on how to run a martial arts school. People all across the country came out of the woodwork crying foul. They had been in business 20 years. They made more money than I did. They were more successful than I was.

The front page story, bottom left helped legitimize my claim quickly and took little effort to arrange!

They knew Chuck Norris, Bruce Lee, or Jackie Chan. Who the hell did I think I was?

But it didn't matter. I had the only book ever published at that time on how to run a martial arts school. Two leading magazines ran feature articles on me and the book. A major supply company started selling the book and within a matter of months I was the de-facto leader in the martial arts business!

I did the very same thing a decade later in the golf business with the identical successful results!

You too can be the leader in your industry in sixty seconds or less by simply announcing that fact to the world!

Don't overcomplicate your marketing. Make a bold claim, make it before anyone else in your industry, then put the tools in place to back it up as you move forward!

CHAPTER 108

Once You Are on a DVD, You Are on TV!

One important fact to remember in personal marketing is that once you have produced a DVD and someone puts it in a machine and hits play, you are now on TV. It doesn't matter what it cost you to film it, you are up there just like Tom Cruise! Being on that screen is an incredibly powerful tool in self-branding.

In the late Nineties I was able to produce a pretty decent 30-minute show called *Martial Arts Business Magazine* for just $1,500 a month. The show was quick paced and patterned after *PM Magazine*. It was mailed out to paying customers as part of our monthly program, but was also used to solicit new business.

Later I did a series of 12 videos on how to run a martial arts school. These made money while increasing my reputation as the world's leading authority on the subject.

These days I film some of my marketing boot camps. The clips can be used on my website and in boxed sets of the whole event that I give to the participants so they can go home and share the concepts with others. While I don't make money off people who watch my boot camp without showing up, I do generate a large amount of business from it without ever having to show up either!

Film your sales demo, seminar, or insights. Get someone to

interview you with a series of questions that positions you well in your industry. Then edit it all into your own show!

The celebrity power of being on someone's TV screen cannot be overstated, even if you got there via a self-produced DVD!

CHAPTER 109

Top 10 Ways to Quickly Enhance Your Personal Brand and Industry Status!

This is a bulletproof blueprint for getting to the top of your profession, organized by the amount of time, money, and effort it takes to accomplish each task.

1. **Blog** – A quick, easy, cheap, effective way to get your knowledge and expertise out to clients and prospects.

2. **E-newsletter** – Takes more time but can quickly build a loyal following.

3. **Speaking** – Not everyone can do it well, but it's a very powerful tool. If you can't speak well, take lessons. Speak wherever you can!

4. **Free special report or booklet** – Easy, effective, and you can get someone else to write it using your ideas if you have trouble getting them down on paper.

5. **Articles** – The more articles you get out in your industry, the more quickly your reputation will grow. Make sure all your articles have a resource box with a short bio and a link back to your website!

6. **Free audio** – Takes some time and some money but a very effective way to market.

7. **Get yourself on radio or TV** – Takes time and effort but can be a great boost, and it's easier to do than most people think.

8. **DVD** – Don't leave getting on TV to chance. Create your own show, get someone to watch it, and it's mission accomplished. Not as expensive as you would think.

9. **Book** – Takes time, effort, and money, but perhaps is the most prestigious and longest-lasting tool to build your personal reputation. (You can always hire a ghostwriter.)

10. **Sophisticated website incorporating all of the above** – This takes time, money, and effort, but you can incorporate almost all of the above elements into one website so people can watch you, listen to you, read your articles, and interact with you!

Work through this list from start to finish and you will have legendary status in your industry.

CHAPTER 110

Standing Out from the Crowd with a Personal Signature

From rock stars to Realtors, entrepreneurs to athletes, having personal signatures, gestures, and style can help build a personal brand quickly, bringing additional income and opportunities along with it.

Famous golfer Gary Player stood out from the crowd and significantly increased his marketing value by becoming the "Black Knight." Player originally wore white outfits to reflect the sun and keep cooler. When he changed to all black, he told reporters he did it to absorb the sun's energy. But the truth of the matter was that it made him easily identifiable, even at a distance. It became his trademark. A similar style also worked for Johnny Cash.

When I started Legendary Marketing in 1998, I decided to use orange as our signature color. It was bright, it stood out, and at that time I couldn't find one major company using that color. It worked. Soon partners and prospects alike were calling our bright orange polo shirts Legendary Orange!

Stephen Jobs of Apple fame has his black crewneck shirt and jeans, while Bill Gates has his glasses. Richard Branson has his beard. Others opt for bow ties, different hair styles (Trump), and power ties.

Generals also used little tools like this to build a reputation. Patton wore a steel helmet and six-shooters on both hips while MacArthur sported a flat cap, sunglasses, and a corncob pipe. Both generals stood out a mile and used their headgear and accessories as a kind of trademark for their personalities.

Churchill had his ever-present cigar and his V-for-victory sign. Einstein was defined by his cloud of gray hair. Ghandi by his simple white garment and round, steel eyeglasses. All of these people at the top of their professions understood the effect of using these seemingly insignificant symbols, colors, and gestures as a way to increase their power, charisma, and personal brand!

Having a color, symbol, accessory, or style that is unique to you will help you stand out in a crowded marketplace!

CHAPTER 111

How to Become an Instant Author

There are few things as strong for personal branding as writing a book! But let's face it, not everyone has the time, ability, or inclination to write one. If you just don't have a book in you, you can still benefit from a much simpler form of publishing. Write a short 5–10 page booklet on your specific field of expertise. Have a graphics house design a nice layout, print it up, and give it away to anyone who will take one.

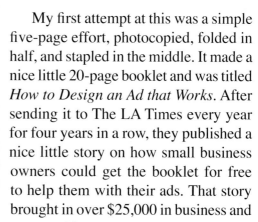

My first attempt at this was a simple five-page effort, photocopied, folded in half, and stapled in the middle. It made a nice little 20-page booklet and was titled *How to Design an Ad that Works*. After sending it to The LA Times every year for four years in a row, they published a nice little story on how small business owners could get the booklet for free to help them with their ads. That story brought in over $25,000 in business and made a nice addition to my press kit.

I have used this tactic many times in many different fields. Sometimes I write them for my clients, other times I have people write them for me. Booklets always make a big impression on people and help build your reputation.

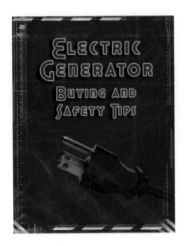

If you are a golf pro, write a booklet on 10 ways to stop a slice. If you are a chiropractor, write a booklet on the 12 ways to avoid back trouble. It you are an attorney, write a booklet on what to do if you are involved in an accident.

If you are a big corporation, as many of my clients are, you can use this tactic to show your clients you care about them. One of the major insurance companies I worked with published a whole series of booklets to help their clients improve their businesses. Not one had anything to do with insurance, but all had something to do with building the company's reputation as an insurance carrier that cared about the success of their clients.

Getting Your Booklet Out

Once your booklet is published, the next trick is to get it

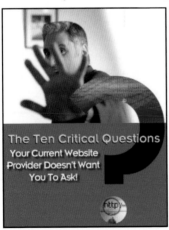

out so it attracts the attention you desire. Start by giving booklets out to all your existing customers and asking them to pass the information along to a friend. Next look for others who are strategically aligned to your business. We got hospitals and doctors offices to give away our booklets on building self-esteem in children. I got speakers bureaus to give out my booklet *A Meeting Planner's Guide to*

Successful Events, and even customized the booklets with the individual bureaus' phone numbers on them.

We had banks, toy stores, and hairdressers give away our booklets on building confidence in kids. The possibilities for distribution are as endless as your imagination. Also, don't forget the press when it comes to your booklet. Let them know it's available to help their readers with their choices, problems, and businesses by sending them a copy along with a professional press release.

Booklets are a quick, easy, and cheap way to showcase your knowledge in print and build your professional reputation!

CHAPTER 112

24 Realtors — Hmmm...Which Should I Choose!?

A few years ago, I was thinking about selling my home. The prices at the time were rising rapidly in California, which would leave me with a tidy profit. On top of that, I had a very interesting opportunity to buy a beautiful piece of property out of state. Things on the new property had not yet been finalized, so I simply decided to stick a For Sale sign in front of my house to see if the interest was there at the price I wanted.

Within two or three days of putting out a For Sale by Owner sign, I was swamped with calls from local real estate agents, 24 in all. They left business cards on my door and sent me flyers, notepads, refrigerator magnets, and handwritten notes. They all said basically the same thing, "Call me, I want to list your property."

Several even followed up with phone calls that ranged in manner from "Hi, I have never met you but I know we are going to be great friends," to a point blank, "Let me have your listing. I'm the best."

They all told me that they were the area's specialists and had sold more houses than anyone else that month, week, year, or decade, depending on which period best suited their needs. They told me how they were the top people in their office or members of the Million Dollar Club — whatever that was. They informed me that I need not speak to anyone else.

Only one person out of the twelve or so who continued to seek the listing showed any interest in my wants and needs whatsoever. One lady actually took the trouble to put together a little package of information on my house, and it was hand delivered to my home. She showed me the previous selling price, tax rates, a detailed description of the property, and an overview of the area's schools, churches, shops, and services. In other words, she clearly demonstrated to me that she knew all about the area in which she sold. She also included the selling prices on several other similar homes in the area, complete with pictures of them so I could compare them. She even had a little graph showing the price trends and had also included information about helping the potential buyers get financing quickly. At the end of the package was a warm friendly letter and an invitation to call for anything else I needed to make a decision on which agent to use should I, in fact, decide to list the property with an agent.

The package was spiral bound and covered in card stock. On the front, she had placed a label with my name typed in bold letters. Now it doesn't take much thought to know which Realtor I would call. As it happened, I decided not to move, but I recommended that Realtor to several other people and I know she got some business from them.

It cost her very little money to photocopy a few pages of information. The information she gave me was available to all the Realtors in the area. When they asked me to let them make several thousands of dollars by listing my home with them, only one went to the trouble to actually market herself to me.

This is a perfect example of how poorly some so-called professionals market themselves and their products or services.

Expertise, experience, and skill don't mean much if you can't market them effectively.

Make the extra effort to stand out from your peers. It's usually not that hard!

i2

Ninja

Marketing

CHAPTER 113

Stealth Marketing Techniques So Cunningly Clever Your Competitors Will Pull Out Their Hair!

Have you got a competitor that just rubs you the wrong way? Someone who you know badmouths you behind your back yet treats you like a long-lost friend at every convention you attend? Or perhaps you have a former partner, client, or employee who snuck off in the middle of the night with your customer list and whatever business he could plunder?

Yes, my friend, these tactics are for YOU, chosen for their effectiveness, cunning, and guile!

Now, stealth marketing is not for everyone. You may find that some of these ideas are just not the type of tactics you would use. BUT...they *are* different and they do work.

Even if you don't like an idea the first time you read it, think about it, kick it around, and just maybe you'll find a way to use the *concept* to your advantage even if the exact *tactic* is not for you.

Very often you will find that your most significant BREAK-THOUGH IDEAS are ones you come up with on your own after being stimulated to think or look at something in a different way.

Use techniques that have been successful in other industries and adapt them to your own needs!

CHAPTER 114

Taking Out Your Competition with a Bottle of Dom Perignon

Many years ago when I ran my karate school, an athletic young man from New Zealand made several visits to my school without signing up. Each time he asked for information that bore no relationship to wanting to study and a strong relationship to wanting to open a karate school. Still, I treated the guy with guarded respect and courtesy. Sure enough, about three weeks later he opened a school a couple of miles away.

Now in the karate business, the typical reaction to a new competitor is — to say the least — not very positive. I went by his school and saw at once that the school was far too large and was in a poor location. It had no chance from day one. Instead of acting angry and hurt, I did just the opposite of what he probably expected. I stopped by the school and left him a bottle of Dom Perignon and a card wishing him well. He had not been there when I stopped by but he called me later to thank me and express his astonishment about my attitude.

Six months later when he went out of business, he sent all fifty of the students he had signed up to my school. That bottle of champagne may be the best $100 I ever spent to get business.

While it's not always possible, keeping good relations with your competitors can result in better business for both of you. Why not be the first to reach out? Refer each other business you can't take or don't want. Take a booking fee for your trouble or just keep score on a quid pro quo basis.

You catch more bees with honey than vinegar!

CHAPTER 115

Tricks of the Trade Shows

There's No Place Like Home — Your Home Page, That Is

At a convention in Palm Springs, I slipped into the hotel's business center and changed the home pages from the hotel's site to Legendary Marketing's home page on all six of the computers. Apparently no one knew how to switch them back (a two-second exercise) because, although they posted a sign asking that people not change the default settings the next day, no one had bothered to change them back. My home page was left up on all of their business center computers for the three-day duration of the convention.

It was great visibility and brought more than a few good leads. I stood in the corner of the room watching a couple of my competitors log into their email accounts; I guess they thought I must have sponsored the home page because they never touched it!!!

Putting your home page as the default at a trade show gives you "guerrilla" visibility.

A Value-Added Gift for My Competitors, Prospects, and Clients

At another industry show, a couple of my staff stood outside the room where speeches on marketing were taking place and handed out my free marketing CDs to the people walking out. They left before the speaker and his entourage exited (that would have been tacky). We got a number of clients from that simple effort and several even commented on hearing me speak at the show — which I didn't!

You can promote yourself at the expense of your competitors.

Don't Miss Booth 213!

At another trade show we gave everyone who walked by — and would take one — a bright orange sticker that said **Don't Miss Booth 213!** For their trouble, they got entered into an hourly drawing for a free vacation worth $1,500! By the second day, over half the convention attendees were wearing the stickers promoting our booth!

Ouch! That's got to hurt when they are standing there talking to a competitor! The real fun, of course, is the number of people who actually walk over to the booth and say "Okay, everyone tells me I ought to talk with you guys — what have you got?"

At trade shows in particular, if you want to get maximum visibility and value among the clutter, it's wise to heed the immortal words of Virgil who said...

Fortune favors the bold!

CHAPTER 116

Sponsor Yourself to Success

Here is a great little tactic that brought more than 1,000 eager prospects to my door for less than $50!!! For a decade now, I have spoken to the 42 chapters of a particular trade association. Most years I spoke three or four times and charged them $3,000–$6,000 plus expenses. That was a bargain as my normal fees are $10,000 and up, but the money I made on the back end by selling websites and services more than made up for the lower fee.

The problem was that for a long time the association had sponsorships to pay my fee and suddenly that money went away. Now I could have offered just to speak for FREE, it would still have been worth it for me — but where is the cunning cleverness in that?

Instead I wrote a letter to each of the association chapter heads offering to speak for $10,000 a day, plus expenses. I also mentioned that thanks to a contact I had with another company (one I own), they were willing to pay my fee for the association as long as they could be mentioned at the event.

Within a week I had booked ten speaking engagements and they still picked up my travel. It was a thing of beauty, an eight-hour seminar to showcase my knowledge to 100 plus people in 10 states and it cost me 42 stamps and paper!

The directors got to look good by bringing in sponsorship and a top speaker. The members got an information-packed seminar, and I got to sell. It was the perfect win, win, win situation.

Competitors in this industry wanted to speak to these associations as well BUT...according to a couple of the chapter heads, they couldn't provide any sponsorship!

Can you provide sponsorship to get in front of your audience?

CHAPTER 117

Customers Want Recognition!
Give It to Them!

For sheer cunningness, longevity, goodwill, and income generated, this may be my most cunningly clever idea ever!

I was coming home from doing a martial arts business seminar in Dallas. It had gone very well but I was still struggling to hit critical mass with my business. My first annual Mastermind Weekend was fast approaching and I had made the glorious mistake of offering the two-day seminar as a bonus to my clients for signing up for my monthly consulting program. I was looking at a $20,000 expense with $3,000 in the bank. I was thinking about this PROBLEM on the plane as I was thumbing through a copy of a golf magazine, which happened to be their annual issue of top 100 clubs.

BINGO!

What if I presented awards for the top 100 karate schools? After all, I owned the only magazine in the industry. As soon as I got off the plane, I contacted all the top organizations and asked them to send me a list of their top ten schools, ones that were, because of their size, longevity, and value to the industry, the best of the best. Some cooperated, many did not. But by including a bunch of people I knew, I rounded up not 100 but 200 names.

I sent out a letter inviting each of the two hundred instruc-

People love to be recognized for their achievements, make that fact work with your customers and clients!

tors to collect their awards at a banquet in Palm Springs. If they wished, while they were there they could attend the extended Mastermind Weekend (I added two days to the FREE convention) for just $199.

Amazingly, over 200 people showed from all over the country — 99% of them attended the convention and most brought guests for the awards banquet. In addition to the launch of the Master Club (detailed in another chapter), we sold over $20,000 worth of manuals and tapes on the final day!

The event also attracted large numbers of people from the ranks of my three or four biggest competitors — almost all of whom became *my* customers in the following months!

Backed by the strength of the *Top 200* awards, and later the *Top 500* awards, the convention grew from 200, to 500, to 700, to 900 before eventually peaking at 1,500 participants! Several of the events made over $100,000 while the residual business they generated was amazing!

But the funny thing is, none of it would have worked if it were not for the awards! Just the other day a member of my staff told me he went into a local karate school and the instructor still proudly displayed his plaque on the wall more than a decade later!

People love recognition!
If you can find a way to get that concept into your marketing, it can only be good!

CHAPTER 118

Fish Where the Fish Are If You Want to Eat Tonight!

I showed up at my karate school one Saturday morning to find there was almost no one there. This was highly unusual since it was our busiest day. "Where is everyone?" I asked my instructor. "Down at the new car wash," he said jokingly. But sure enough I had just driven past it and it was jam-packed with people.

I got back in my car and sought out the manager who told me that over 1,000 people would visit on an average weekend. Since they had nothing to do for 15 to 20 minutes, I asked him whether I could set up a booth in front of the office and give out free promo items for my karate school. He immediately agreed — after I set his six-year-old son up with free lessons.

With a captive audience seeking something to do, or at least someone to talk with, we never once left the car wash without signing up a new student.

Simple yet effective!

You can sell memberships, vacations, and chiropractic, spa, or beauty services more effectively from a booth in a crowded mall than waiting in your office for people to walk in the door! You can sell vehicles of all kinds in a stadium parking lot with 75,000 people walking by! Set up shop at a football game, a swap meet, a local fair, a mall, a church, or wherever large crowds of people will be!

**If the customers aren't coming to you,
go wherever they happen to be!**

CHAPTER 119

Uncovering Your Competitor's Customers in a Matter of Minutes

Other than your own customer list, the next most valuable list is your competitors' customers. They have people who are already proven buyers who, given the right reason or right offer, will switch to you!

But first you have to find them.

In some states you can run people's license plates online as a matter of public record. In others, it's illegal. So is asking a member of the police, fire, or ambulance services to run the numbers for you. But it's not illegal everywhere and a friend at the DMV could go a long way — wink, wink!

Anyway, a friend of mine told me that he went around to all the local golf clubs he competed against and took pictures of the cars in the parking lots with his cell phone. When he got back to his club "someone" he knew ran all the plates and got their mailing addresses. He built a large and VERY targeted mailing list of Grade A prospects in six weeks.

The response according to him was spectacular!

Depending on your business, there are all kinds of intriguing ways to find your competitors' clients.

Real estate closings, new car registrations, and other government filings are a huge source of competitive data. You just have to know where to look in your industry. Well, that and actually taking the time to look!

CHAPTER 120

B2B Customers Lists Are Even Easier to Find!

In a business-to-business environment it is usually not very hard at all to find your competitors' clients. For example, a lot of service providers like ad agencies actually list their clients on their websites. You can find a web company's clients just by googling their name and following all the links.

It astonishes me that more companies don't do this, but a simple, quick, and cheap way to find out who your competitors' customers are serviced by is simply to call people you'd like as customers and ask!

Ask whomever answers the phone, "Who is your current insurance company?" (uniform supplier, security company, or whatever) and nine times out of ten they will tell you. You then know who your competition is.

Look for creative ways of finding your competitors' clients. It's the second most valuable list you will ever own!

CHAPTER 121

Free Product Uncovers Competitors' Clients with Devastating Effect!

One of the key ways to get your competitors' customers to identify themselves is simply to give away your product or service for free. I give away free seminars on CD. Hotels offer a free room. At golf courses, a free round. With professional or management services, it's a free consultation.

The key is to make sure that when they register on your website to get their free gift, one of the questions you ask is who they are doing business with now. If you provide a list all of your competitors so they can check off who they use, so much the better as it will be easier to sort later.

In one promotion we did for a top resort, 5,000 people signed up for a free room. Of those, 953 identified themselves as people who had never stayed at the resort but who had frequented a leading competitor. We pulled the list of 953 people, wrote a one-page sales letter, included an audio book as a gift, and invited them to book a vacation with the resort.

The campaign had an astonishing 63% response rate. Think about that — not 0.5%, not 1% or 2%, but 63%! Results like this are why it's so important to uncover your competitors' customers and preach to them. They are the most highly qualified prospects you can get as they are already paying for a product or service similar to what you offer.

In another case where we offered free golf, we built a list of almost 10,000 people in just over a month. From that list we were able to get just under 10% to book a round after their free game, all of whom had identified other clubs as their primary courses. That's $65,000 in green fees from a single email blast! (But only after we had identified our competitors' customers and customized a targeted offer for them.)

Use freebies to get your competitors' customers to identify themselves on your website. Then follow up with a custom campaign!

CHAPTER 122

Yellow Pages Savvy Increases Calls by 500% While Decreasing Ad Size 50%!

A few years ago I advised one of my clients in the retail/whole-sale supply business to run a smaller ad in the Yellow Pages — an ad that was 50% smaller in size than the one he had been running for years with decreasing response and rising ad rates.

The results astonished him. Despite the lack of any graphics, his address — or even his business name — his calls increased by 500%.

My advice was that instead of competing by going head to head with the numerous other competitors in the greater Los Angles area, he ought to outsmart them. The solution was to place a small box ad with a large headline and bold 800 number offering a free referral service.

Hundreds of people called him first when looking for supplies. If they lived close to his business he, of course, sent them there. If not, he either referred them to another business, enhancing his reputation among his customers and peers, or in a few cases if it was a large order he would sell the lead.

Either way he was a winner!

This can work for any service business such as doctors, dentists, chiropractors, lawyers, accountants, limousine services, and more. Now, of course, you can also do the same thing on the web.

Starting a referral service for your business category can usurp a lot of calls from your competition!

CHAPTER 123

Getting Other Businesses to Willingly Attract New Customers for You!

Gift certificates are one of those tried-and-tested ideas that we sometimes forget about as a marketing tool. Sure, you use them at Christmas, but what about the rest of the year? Here are a couple of excellent ways to put a different twist on using gift certificates — and enjoy the extra income all year long by giving them away rather than actually selling them to your customers.

The first step is to seek out compatible stores for your particular business. A golf pro working at a driving range might target local golf shops. In the karate business we targeted party stores, toy shops, pizza parlors, and other places where kids and families hung out. A clothing store might target a shoe shop or a dry cleaner. A service station might target an auto parts store. Who you choose will depend on your demographics and your product or service.

How many gift certificates you give the store is entirely up to you, because the purpose is to get your gift certificates in the hands of prospective clients who meet your basic demographic profile. The gift certificates should be high-end, really good-looking certificates, ones that look like they are really valuable and not some second-rate photocopied coupon.

How to Solicit Other Businesses to Come to Your Aid

Get to the person in charge of your target business and tell them this. How would you like to provide your best clients with an extra bonus of X dollars for every purchase they make over $100, $500, $1,000 — whatever makes sense for your product? Then you can either wait for his response or let the person know at once that you're not trying to sell him anything, just offering him a win-win business promotion. Once he agrees to the concept of providing his best clients with additional value at no cost, you can offer him as many gift certificates as you wish. Make sure that the merchant understands this is a no-strings-attached offer for him and his clients, and you will more often than not meet with success.

Let's say you own a dry cleaning store. How about going to all the dress shops and men's stores within three miles of your business and giving each of them 20 free $10 gift certificates that they can give away as a value-added service for any client who spends over $200? Now, how many of them do you think are going to turn down that offer?

No one in business with a brain, anyway! (Which means as many as two thirds might turn it down!)

Now, how many new faces will that bring into your store? Plenty! Then it's up to you to treat them right and turn them into full-fledged customers. Chiropractors could give gift certificates to local health clubs, golf clubs, and tennis clubs. Dentists could give a free checkup certificate to local preschools, and so on. The possibilities are limited only by your imagination.

The key is to remember that this is not merely a discount coupon, but an actual gift certificate that is being added to a sale in recognition of a substantial purchase, or because that person has been a loyal client. This creates a huge perceived difference in whether or not the certificate is actually redeemed.

Here's the kicker — you can often get businesses located close to your competitors' locations to participate and drive business to you since your competitors weren't smart enough to have ever asked them! Often I had to correct people who called to make an appointment on where our location was as they often assumed I was the business in the same plaza where they had been given the certificate rather than just down the street!

What About the Cost?

If the thought of giving product or service away bothers you, look at it this way. If you run a full-page ad in your local *Penny Saver* or coupon mailer, it's going to cost you five or six hundred dollars and you still can't guarantee any new business. If you give away sixty $10 gift certificates to your dry cleaner, you are virtually assured of getting new business. What's more, it only costs you ten dollars for the certificates that actually come back! And remember, they'll probably spend more than the value of the gift certificates so you may break even or make a profit on the first transaction.

Let's say that half the certificates are redeemed by people who are already your customers and half who are not. That means it costs you $20 per new customer, which is incredibly cheap customer acquisition over the lifetime of a typical customer in most businesses. Think of this type of program as an alternative to advertising — only with far better results since you only pay for the leads you actually get!

Use gift certificates as a cheap way to acquire customers as well as a way to make money!

CHAPTER 124

Enlisting Friends and Family to Come to Your Aid

Another way to distribute gift certificates is to get your existing clients to distribute them to their friends and family. Every Christmas we used to send all the students in my karate schools two free $80 gift certificates (the price of a month's lessons). Along with the cards was a letter letting them know that the gift certificates could be passed along to friends as a gift and would be treated as such when their friends arrived at the school.

The letter also pointed out that the certificates were only redeemable for lessons and that they could not be used by existing students. Sometimes the students asked if the certificates could be used by another person in their family, which we of course allowed because after a month they became regular paying clients.

Think about this if you are a heath spa, chiropractor, acupuncturist, or just about any service provider — you should get a decent number of referrals, normally about 20%! What do you think your rate will be if you give every customer a gift certificate valued at $100 to pass on to a friend? 50%? 60%? 80%?

Whatever the number is, it will be double or triple the standard referral rate and gives you the added benefit of goodwill with your existing customers!

Getting existing customers to gift their friends brings a lot of new business and a lot of goodwill, for almost nothing!

i3

Marketing
Sabotage

CHAPTER 125

Why Personal Prejudice Destroys Most Brilliant Marketing Campaigns Before They Even Start!

Everyone has an opinion about marketing. Unfortunately, rarely is that opinion based on fact or real-world experience backed by actual results. Instead it is almost always based on personal preference for color or style. Many opinions are also based on myths that have been handed down for decades and repeated so many times that they are now WRONGLY considered to be FACT by 99% of the world.

Most importantly, since the people judging your marketing are rarely the same people you are actually trying to attract, their opinion on your marketing is basically worthless! Worthless because their opinion is based, not on marketing science, but on their own social, economic, and psychological preferences, which are rarely the same as those of the people you are trying to attract!

Make no mistake about it, 99% of the time people judge your work based on what they like or think they know about marketing, not on what will actually work!

The key to great marketing is not to design marketing that people like. It is to design marketing that motivates targeted prospects to action. Whomever your target market is, it is a very tiny percentage of the entire population. They are a certain age, have certain hobbies, wants, needs, and passions. If the people who make marketing decisions are not part of that particular lifestyle, it's very unlikely that their opinions will be accurate.

For example, in the golf resort business, if marketing directors are not avid golfers they cannot possibly understand the emotional connection that a good ad will have with an avid golfer. Just as I can't possibly understand why my wife enjoys mucking out horse stables and riding the beasts. (Never take up a hobby in which the main party eats while you sleep!) Nor, unless marketing directors have exceptional marketing experience, are they qualified to provide any useful input on the ads in question. But they will anyway!

A great deal of the best marketing we have ever produced has never seen the light of day because it does not meet the criteria of the person paying the bills — or, worse still, the assistant he has entrusted to make judgments on marketing matters!

Before you hire anyone to design a marketing campaign, educate yourself. Read a good book. Share this one, but feel free to cross reference with others. Discover the real principles of marketing from a true leader in the field, not from someone who happens to run a small design company down the street or works for a big agency with marble floors who has NEVER spent a dime of his own money on marketing!

Read *Ogilvy on Advertising*. David Ogilvy built the biggest ad agency in the world from scratch. In his book's pages you will discover many things you never knew, like why long copy ALWAYS sells better than short copy. Or get the classic book *Scientific Advertising* by Claude Hopkins, *Marketing Your Services: For People Who Hate to Sell* by Rick Crandall, or just about anything by Dan Kennedy or Jay Abraham! In books like these you will discover that the real secrets of marketing are not what most people think they are; in fact, very often they are the opposite!

Design your marketing to create response, NOT to please your ego, your owner, your staff, your customers, your family, friends, or spouse!

You'll find it far more profitable!

CHAPTER 126

But Everyone Loves My Ad!!!

Several years ago I designed an ad for a well-known manufacturer of carbon-graphite shafts for golf clubs. At the time it was quite simply the best ad I had ever designed.

I used my personal passion for golf and backed up my knowledge with abundant and irrefutable research on what people look for when they buy a golf club.

The VP of marketing who had been in the golf business for many years loved it. So did a host of golfers with whom I tested the ad! BUT the new CEO, a recent graduate from Harvard who didn't play golf, wasn't sure. He said, and I quote, "I'm not getting a warm, fuzzy feeling about it!"

To set his mind at ease, he left the conference room, which adjoined the manufacturing plant, and entered the factory. There I watched in complete disbelief as he wandered from worker to worker, of whom 50% spoke no English and the other 50% suffered from the effects of too much glue sniffing, and showed them the ad.

Five minutes later he returned and announced, "The boys don't get it!"

The boys don't get it because the boys don't play golf. The boys don't get it because their idea of fun is shooting coyotes as they run back and forth across the Mexican border.

Hello!

He simply didn't get it. He wanted the workers to feel good about the ad; he didn't want an ad that would work!

Unfortunately this is true in many, many businesses. Owners, CEOs, and marketing executives who don't know the first thing about advertising make terrible decisions based on what *they* like, not what *the customer* is looking for or will respond to!

Customers buy only two things: benefits and solutions. They do not buy features. They do not buy because of your logo, because your picture happens to be in the ad, or because you have been in business for 20 years. They only care about what your business or product can do for them.

After my first ad for the shaft maker was rejected, I came back with another that offered information to people in the club-fitting business who were among the prime buyers of their shafts. This time the CEO turned down the idea because he feared it might generate too much interest and clog up the company's antiquated phone system!

I resigned after that one.

Your marketing should be written and designed only for one specific type of person, no one else. What anyone but those targeted prospects think of your copy or design does not matter one iota!

In fact, if lots of unqualified people look at the ad and like it, it's an almost sure sign that the ad is not speaking to your target audience in an emotional and personal enough way to be effective. It's almost like "they" should be the only ones who get it! This is true no matter who your target market is, from fishermen to farmers, from toddlers to seniors.

The number one goal of a good ad,
sales letter, brochure, or website is to connect with
a specific targeted prospect and motivate *that*
person to action.

No one else matters!

CHAPTER 127

In the Land of the Blind, the One-Eyed Man Is King!

I'm sitting in the elegant boardroom of a large company with the CEO on one end and me on the other. Between us are his team of managers and marketing advisors.

"Andrew," he says, "We like your web work but we are not sure about your print capabilities. We have seen your stuff and, to be honest we really don't like it. What we do like is collateral like this." He announces this as he pushes a high-gloss brochure from his leading competitor down the table.

I look the brochure over quickly; it's typical agency stuff — long on style, short on content, and, most importantly, **worthless at generating response.**

"So," I say carefully, "if I understand you correctly, Mr. CEO, what you would like me to do is design marketing material for your prospects, most of whom are over 65 years old, that looks good but that none of your prospects will ever read!"

There was silence for a minute, then unable to solve the puzzle one of the marketing people said, "Are you trying to be funny, Andrew? Because, if so, I think we all missed the joke."

"No, I'm not trying to be funny. I am trying to understand if you want me to produce response or just produce worthless brochures that look like those of your competitors," I said as I pushed the brochure back down the table at the CEO, who was around 48 years old. "Go ahead and read the first few lines to us if you would," I asked softly.

He picked the brochure up, opened the first page and... silence.

He passed the brochure to the marketing lady on his right. She studied it for a while and passed it over to the manager, and so it went down the table until it came to me. While my eyesight is not the best at a distance, I have no problem with small type even if it's only 8-point, reverse type on a sepia background.

I was the ONLY person in the room who could read that brochure and I'm 20 years younger than their target market.

Fancy type styles, background images, shading, and special paper treatments are all great, but if your prospects can't EASILY read your message, you won't sell a thing!

CHAPTER 128

A Strange Visit to Budget Fantasyland

Perhaps the simplest way to sabotage your marketing is to enter into it without a proper "backwards-based budget." Marketing plans don't run on air, but seldom is a proper plan in place to match goals to the marketing budget.

You must have a realistic budget to get serious marketing results.

This means...

- You cannot set a marketing budget based on a percentage of your gross or net.

- You cannot set a marketing budget based on what your competition does or "industry averages."

- Nor can you allot what you can afford or, as many businesses do, simply pull a number out of your head.

Based on thousands of conversations, I think the majority of business owners must throw darts to determine their budgets!

The only way you can set the right marketing budget is to reverse engineer exactly what you want to happen.

The step-by-step process outlined here will allow you to look at budgeting and meeting budgeting goals in a powerful new way

— a way that directly connects everything you do in the name of marketing to a specific and tangible result.

A great many business owners must really like fantasy movies; they want to sell 50 real-estate lots with a $20,000 budget! Or they want a 20% increase in product sales with a budget that's based on 5% of last year's miserable gross!

You cannot increase business by spending less on marketing, although you don't always have to spend more to get the results you want. Often it's just a case of spending where the response is greatest and NOT spending where there is no direct or tangible return.

If you want to sell 100 lots, 100 products, or 100 hours of your service you cannot do it by arbitrarily picking a number for your marketing budget. You have to ask: How many leads must you generate to sell 100 lots?

To answer that question, you need to know what percentage of leads your salespeople close.

If you expect the salesperson to sell one out of five prospects, that means you need to generate 500 leads to sell 100 lots.

So how many leads does your $4,000 glossy ad bring in — seven or eight? Not enough. Perhaps you should look at direct mail.

At a 1% rate of response you will need to send 50,000 letters to generate 500 leads. At a 2% response rate, it's 25,000 letters, envelopes, stamps, and time. Let's say the mailings come to $25,000, or a dollar apiece, when all is said and done.

This is $10,000 more than the proposed budget and you still have no idea if the salesperson you just hired can actually sell a drunk a beer! All you have done so far is generate the number of leads needed to sell 100 lots. However, this is a step taken only by about 0.1% of businesses.

I'm not saying you have to spend more, just that you have to have a realistic plan. Put a number on every piece of marketing you do with a cost and an estimate of how many leads each medium will generate.

- billboards

- Yellow Pages

- website

- radio

- TV

- referrals

- telemarketing

This year it might be a guess, but next year you will know for sure and will be able to do a budget that matches leads to sales to goals!

Brilliant!

The only logical way to determine an effective marketing budget is to work it backwards from your sales goal. How many leads will it take to reach that goal and how much will it cost to generate that many leads?

Any other way of budgeting is pure fantasy!

CHAPTER 129

Seduction by Numbers

Thousands of ad salespeople make a living by seducing business owners and marketing mangers with large numbers. It boggles my mind when I talk to a partner looking for 100 customers. They're running ads statewide, even nationwide, in numerous glossy magazines that total 3 million readers when they are in fact looking for 100 people willing to spend, say, $75,000 on a membership and perhaps a half a million on a home. The theory is that a certain percentage of people who read your ad will respond.

That, my friend, is simply not true!

In a 100-page magazine, only a tiny fraction of the readers will ever see your full-page ad, with the picture of the signature home in a section that has 12–16 pages of similar ads. Maybe only 1% will read your smaller ad.

Successful marketing is, and always will be, about reaching *targeted* prospects.

A targeted mailing list of 5,000 prospects would be 70% cheaper and about 1000% more effective than mass advertising in the newspaper to 100,000 people, but that small number just throws people off. They think BIG is better, when, in fact, targeted is better! That means targeted mailings, targeted emails, and targeted websites.

If you ran an ad on a relevant website and got 150 names, addresses, and emails, you would be so far ahead of the game compared to a local newspaper ad that it's not even funny. But most people just don't get it! They think the numbers are too small. Instead they advertise in outlets with large circulations that are not targeted to their product.

Do NOT be seduced by huge circulation numbers. Focus on the *quality* of your leads, not the *quantity*!

CHAPTER 130

Why Perfection Kills
Great Campaigns

I have been putting out an electronic newsletter on marketing for ten years now. There have been some good ones, some great ones, and some truly legendary ones. There have been some very aggressive ones, some controversial ones, and even a few lame ones. Now which do you suppose are the ones that consistently get the most response?

The great ideas, the insightful case histories, or the bold new strategies?

No, none of the above. Despite the fact that my ideas have made people untold millions, the greatest response I get every year to any of my newsletters is to the ones with the most spelling errors or typos!

Readers send me emails saying everything from "You are so unprofessional I would never do business with you or your company" to, "You are an idiot; get a proofreader!"

I write my weekly e-letter and blog on the road from hotel rooms across the world in various time zones. I could send it back to the office to have it proofed and, depending on connectivity, review it the next day. But I could also easily lose a few days in the process. So I choose to give it my best shot and send it out as is, bad grammar and all. Hardly a week goes by when I don't get an email from someone pointing out my misuse of words that spell-check didn't catch.

In the meantime others do read the stuff I send and despite its grammatical shortcomings, they embrace my ideas and become new partners!

I would much rather put my newsletter out every week on time rather than wait and get it proofread and perfect only to go out two days later or not at all that week.

In a perfect world, I could write several e-letters weeks before sending them out and solve my spelling and grammar problems, but creativity doesn't work that way. It comes and goes when it pleases. My point is that by doing something every week, even if it's less than perfect, I gain business.

The point for you is that I can't begin to tell you how many marketing campaigns aren't implemented on schedule because someone on the client's end nitpicks them to death.

I guess that over 50% of the campaigns our company is involved in go out well past their PRIME window of opportunity! Why? Because so and so wants this sentence changed — or two more people have to provide input but one's on vacation and the other just had a hernia! They want three people to proofread it, not one!

In the process, partners in Florida that should have been marketing in the fall, end up doing it in January when the season is already in full swing. TOO LATE!

At every stage of your marketing effort there are people looking to slow you down — people looking for perfection in an imperfect world!

I'm not the only one with this bias. Tom Peters called it a bias for action and said that Ready, Fire, Aim is better than Ready, Aim, Aim, Aim...

Check the web address and phone number three times and don't worry too much about the rest. People agonize over paper stock and insist on getting three quotes when the first quote they get is the best they have ever had. They stop the presses waiting for a new photo shoot when stock art or Photo Shop would have done the trick!

Let others struggle with the vice of perfection — get your marketing out! Just make sure the phone number and web address are correct!

CHAPTER 131

Use Speed as Your Strategy!

Two people whose books influenced me early in my career and made me err on the side of speed were Brian Tracy and Mark McCormick. Both men believed that most great ideas are killed or copied by others while people pursue perfection. A good idea executed quickly, even if it is less than perfect, will massively outperform a perfect piece that goes out six months later. In addition, you'll get months' worth of leads that much earlier. Hey, if you can be fast *and* perfect, so much the better. Just be FAST first!

Let me give you a world-class example of this theory in action! Microsoft NEVER releases a perfect product — in fact, far from it. Instead, it works quickly to develop new technologies it then releases to John Q. Public and lets him find all the bugs so the company can fix them. That's even cheaper than outsourcing the debugging offshore because it's FREE!

Now I am sure that Microsoft wishes it could put out a perfect product, but it also realizes that being ahead of its competitors in launching products is far more important than having a perfect product!

The bottom line is this — if you have a good idea or a need for new clients, get in gear and get something going. Do it on a small scale if you have to, so you can make changes inexpensively later if need be. BUT don't drag out the process for weeks in search of perfection. While you are busy working on choosing the perfect type font, your competition has already licked the stamps on their latest campaign and is heading for the post office.

Speed is a great strategy. Make it yours!

CHAPTER 132

Are You Wasting Your Marketing Money?

What I am going to say may upset you, but I'm going to be frank. If you listen with an open mind, I think by the end of these few pages you will agree with my statement. Not only do I think you will agree with it, but I think you will also see a clear solution to your problem. The problem is that, **if you are not tracking your marketing, you are wasting your money!** And without tracking, every time you do another ad, send another letter, or run another commercial, you are throwing good money after bad.

Do You Honestly Track All of Your Marketing?

Few people do and consequently almost no one can tell you honestly whether any particular aspect of the marketing is working or not. Instead what they will tell you is whether sales are up or down. It sounds like the same thing but, of course, it's not. There are a huge number of reasons why short-term income may be up or down, such as the weather. But income in any given week or month is no real indication of whether your long-term marketing is effective.

I love it the first time new clients actually track their ads because they become instant converts to database, response-DRIVEN marketing.

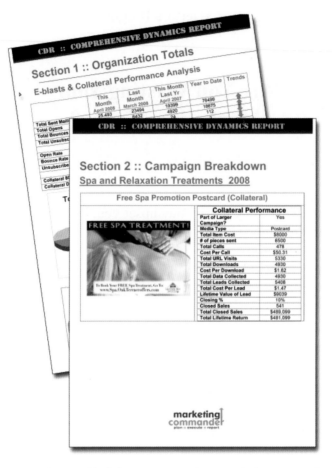

How many phone calls did you generate last month from your ad in the trade magazine, the local newspaper, or a glossy regional magazine? If you do not know the answer to that, you are wasting your money!

Recently, I had a client run a two-page color spread in a local golf magazine with a unique 800 number to track his response. (Marketing Commander tracks this for you automatically and calculates your ROI.) Eight, repeat, eight, people called. The ad cost $12,000 — now that's some expensive marketing and all they were selling were $65 tee times!

But it gets better (actually worse). This was the tenth year they had run the same ad so the ad had actually cost the company $120,000! At least now they won't do it again, but what a waste.

I had another client that ran a $20,000 ad in a major metro newspaper with a circulation of 2 million. They generated just 65 calls although the placement, ad size, and offer were fabulous!

What's even more scary is that prior to tracking their response, they had been spending upwards of $200,000 a year in this publication for almost 20 years! If you are following along and doing the math, that's over four million hard-earned dollars almost completely down the drain!

But heck, it's only money and the newspaper ad salesmen have to feed their families too, so don't feel too bad!

It is the critical task of tracking your marketing that makes Marketing Commander worth its weight in gold. While there may be other solutions out there that do all I am about to describe, I have never found one, so I'm going to tell you about the one my company developed!

With a simple keystroke, or by daily email report sent automatically to your inbox, you can view a Marketing Commander report that tells you instantly which ads, campaigns, and offers are producing responses and which are not.

For example, let's say you run an ad in the local paper for $2,000, while at the same time you send out a postcard campaign. Marketing Commander will separate each and tell you specifically **how many people called for more information from each source**.

Yes, Marketing Commander actually tracks your phone calls! No more asking Becky at the front desk how many people called from your sales-letter campaign, only to get a vague shrug in return. No more scratch pads by the phone used by some employees and ignored by others. No more salespeople fudging on the actual response in order to make their closing ratio look better. (Therein lies one of the great problems in all of marketing — most salespeople, including my own, DON'T WANT TO BE HELD ACCOUNTABLE!)

That's why salespeople, marketing directors, and assistants of every shape and size fight the implementation of new systems, and that's why you have to take the bull by the horns and make it happen.

This is not opinion, it's a common-sense FACT! Running your operation following a carefully orchestrated marketing system that tracks leads from start to finish will produce substantially better results than whatever you are getting now without such as system!

- **How many phone calls does your display ad in the Yellow Pages generate?** If you do not know the answer to that, you are wasting your money!

- **How many phone calls did your last postcard or direct-mail campaign generate?** If you do not know the answer to that, you are wasting your money!

- **How many phone calls did your last radio or TV ad generate?** If you do not know the answer to that, you are wasting your money!

You get the idea!

Once you have looked at the phone traffic for each campaign, you must then look at **how many people visited your website from each individual campaign.**

How many people filled in a contact form, signed up for your offer, or downloaded your sales information from each individual campaign?

With Marketing Commander you can quickly and easily compare the effectiveness of any campaign in real time and calculate your cost per lead. Knowing which offers attract the most business gives you better and better decisions about where to spend your marketing money.

You can load up on the things that work and cut out those things that don't. And please don't tell me you are just building a brand or awareness with your marketing dollars, unless you have millions to spend or have a driving ambition to die BROKE!

You must squeeze every dime you can from your marketing budget and the only way to do this is to track your response. Almost no company can track so effectively because they simply don't have the technology; most are running low-end third-party solutions with their logo stuck on the front. I am not disparaging them, just telling the truth. Call your existing web company and ask them if they can track phone calls through their system and deliver a real time ROI on every marketing campaign you run; they can't.

Marketing Commander was designed from the ground up by people in the sales and marketing business to give our partners a massive competitive edge. The tracking and reporting tools we have are just one of five key areas where the product can help you substantially increase your business.

Now isn't that the type of ADVANTAGE you should be enjoying? Don't think of Marketing Commander as just a website, think of it as your complete marketing command and control center.

I don't care what you use to track your marketing, but track it you MUST! To view a complete demo of our Marketing Commander, go to www.MarketingCommander.com; there is simply nothing like it on the market at the moment.

If you don't track every penny of your marketing, you are throwing money down the drain!

CHAPTER 133

I Have Seen the Enemy and the Enemy Is Me!

I think it was Pogo who said, "We have seen the enemy and he is us." An interesting quote that got me thinking: Why do we stop doing the things that work?

If you ran a specific promo last year to build your database and it worked, why didn't you do it again this year?

If you had a successful sales drive, referral program, or ambassador program last year, why not repeat it this year?

All too often the few marketing strategies that are proven home runs are discarded in favor of trying something new.

Worse still, they are discarded in favor of nothing at all. I suspect we are all guilty of this to some degree. I know that I can think of several things we did last year that were staggeringly successful yet, for no good reason on earth, we didn't repeat them this year.

What have been your most successful offers or strategies in the past?

How could you enhance, update, or refresh those exact same strategies for use in the fall or next spring?

Here's an interesting statistic for you. Let's say you mailed an offer to 10,000 people and 70 responded. In-depth studies show that if you mail the exact same offer, to the exact same list, your response the second time will be exactly 50%. So if 35 people responding makes economic sense, why not get another 10,000 in the mail right away?

Always be looking for creative ways to market BUT don't move on to something else when what you are doing is bringing results!

¡4!

Cunningly Clever Marketing

CHAPTER 134

Selling the World's Most Precious Commodity — Time!

When I lived in Southern California, we used to ski in Big Bear where we had the choice of two resorts. Both were more or less on the same mountain and one was ten dollars a day more than the other. Where would you ski?

I skied Snow Summit, the more expensive of the two. Why? Because they limited ticket sales and had a 10-minute lift-line guarantee! If you were not on a lift in 10 minutes they gave you a ticket for another day free! It never happened. The two or three times I tried the cheaper place, I waited as long as 30 minutes to get up the mountain — NO THANKS!

We used to go to a restaurant around the corner from my office when I lived in California. It had good food and was always packed, but what really made it right for us was they guaranteed your lunch would be on the table in 10 minutes or you didn't pay.

One of the reasons the growth of golf is declining in the US is that it takes too long to play! I have advised a number of my partners to offer **"Play in under 4 hours or your money back!"** That's a bold statement, but I'll tell you what — I'd pay an extra $10 to get that guarantee. With the right course, proper instructions to the players upon check-in, and a good ranger program, it could be done! If you took over four hours to play a round in Scotland — and that's without the aid of a cart — they'd hang you from a lamppost!

As Napoleon once said, "You may ask anything of me except my time!" Time is an important motivator for many people; think how you can use this to your marketing advantage!

**Time can be a great marketing factor.
It's the only thing most people don't
have enough of!**

CHAPTER 135

How to Ethically Clear Out a Bad Product Without Discounting a Dime!

Jon Spoelstra was a marketing consultant and eventual GM of the New Jersey Nets basketball team for three years. He had on his hands the very worst team in the NBA. Not only did they have the worst record of any team in the league, but the players had bad attitudes and the few fans who did show up hated them! So how did the new GM go from a stadium that was not even half full to selling out every game in just a few months, while the team played as badly as ever?

Brilliance, that's how!

Brilliance — and a change in his Unique Selling Proposition. He stopped trying to sell his lousy team. It was pointless — the Nets were terrible and everyone knew it! He couldn't change the quality of play without some serious personnel changes and time to work on things. But he could change the USP and turn the team into a profitable business rather than a money pit. Instead of marketing *his* team, he started to market the stars of the opposition teams.

Come see Michael Jordan and the Chicago Bulls!
Shaq and The LA Lakers!
Larry Bird and the Celtics!

In his favor was the fact that many of the stars he was promoting were nearing the ends of their careers, so he added some of that into the mix. *"This might be your last chance to see Jordan play in New Jersey!"* He bundled the good games into packages of five, tripled the ticket prices for those games and threw in all the mediocre games for free! He sold out the stadium in a matter of weeks while the Nets played as badly as ever! He was no longer selling his team. He was instead selling the superstars on the *opposing teams* as the reason to come to the game. Cunningly Clever marketing at it's finest!

Sometimes you can even save a bad product with great, out-of-the-ordinary marketing!

CHAPTER 136

How a Cartoon Character Grabbed My Heart and Yanked Me by the Wallet into a Bowling Alley 14 Miles Away!

Here is an example of great marketing that caught my fancy. It uses kids to bring adults to a business. Ever since I moved to Citrus County several years ago, I have driven past the Beverly Hills bowling center located just 500 yards from the gates of Black Diamond Ranch where I live. Every time I drove by, I thought to myself that I really ought to take the family there for some fun. But that's where it ended, thinking about it!

They never sent me the traditional new-resident welcome letter. They never invited me down for a free game or sent me anything in the mail suggesting that I hold my kids' birthday parties there. They may well do all of these things but, if they do, nothing has ever crossed my door — or if it has, it simply never stood out enough to get read!

Up until last week I haven't been in a bowling alley for at least a decade — maybe closer to two! But then came a full color, double-sided postcard from Sponge Bob courtesy of Manatee Lanes. For those of you without kids, Sponge Bob is a cartoon character from the Nickelodeon network who lives in a pineapple at the bottom of the sea...but I digress.

Sponge Bob yanked me into the bowing ally with his cunningly clever ploy aimed squarely at my kid!

Sponge Bob invited me to bowl with my son in the Nickelodeon Roll and Bowl league. The 16-week program was a steal for family entertainment at just $15.50 a week. AND… DRUM ROLL, PLEASE…the kid in the equation, in this case my son, gets to keep a Sponge Bob bowling ball and free carrying case! Just in case your kid is not hip enough to think that Sponge Bob is about the coolest little guy on the planet, you can choose from three other cartoon characters.

The original mailing came in about eight weeks ago and, believe me, not a week went by when my son didn't walk into my home office and ask, "Did you call to sign us up yet, Dad? Did you, did you?" Eventually I did — and you know what? We have had a great time, especially after someone pointed out that the miles-per-hour number on the scoring screens that clocks the ball speed is not actually as important as knocking the pins down.

Silly me!

I am pretty sure that the promotion was triggered by my son signing up for access to the Nickelodeon website. That of course made him a very targeted prospect to respond to a Sponge Bob promotion. Anyway, I love the promotion and make the 14-mile round trip to Manatee Lanes every week instead of going to the center right outside the gates.

That, my friends, is proof that good marketing attracts customers — even right from your competitors' own backyards!

Target market to good prospects to "pickpocket" your competitors while they sit back and do nothing!

CHAPTER 137

Cars, Boats, Books, and Bucks —
The Important Art of Getting Paid

Recently I had a proposal for $50,000 of marketing services turned down by a developer. After speaking with the owner I discovered that he was land rich and cash poor. I sent another proposal the following week, only this time I made the proposal for $250,000. This one was for $25,000 in cash and $225,000 in lots; he accepted at once!

In another case I had a small, broke manufacturer want to pay me in product. I spent a small amount of time seeing if I could sell the product, found a buyer in advance, and agreed. In another deal I took 65,000 books as payment flipping all of them at a 100% profit over the trade value in a matter of weeks. I have taken hotel credit, meeting space, water conditioning, Ferrari service, and just about everything in between. Some of the product trades I have put on eBay, turning the trade to cash faster than I would have gotten paid had I sent an invoice!

Many business owners don't want to go to the hassle of barter. But as long as it's a favorable trade, it's really not a bad option since most of your competitors wouldn't dream of doing it! With the advent of eBay and other online selling options, you can turn almost anything into cash quickly. While cash is king, cars, boats, and books are convertible into cash quickly and easily!

One of the quickest and easiest ways to expand your business is to take payment in trade; done right, barter is almost the same as cash!

CHAPTER 138

Getting Paid!
Marketing to Past-Due Accounts

One area that never seems to get any marketing attention is past-due accounts. In fact, other than the effort we have made internally I have NEVER seen any marketing creativity in past-due or demand letters. They are boring, unmotivating, and usually annoying!

It doesn't have to be that way!

In fact you can't afford to have it that way. When someone has failed to pay you in a timely manner, you must use all of your cunningly clever ideas to get them to pay up!

This starts with your collection letter to them.

Instead of the passionless corporate-speak, piece of crap it most likely is now, it should be written with the same passion and effort that your sales letters are. That is, in effect, what it is, a letter selling your client on paying you!

In sending collection letters to our golf partners, one headline referencing golf terms says:

You have just made a bogey, let's not make it a double... and goes on to talk in golf terms about their account!

Be humorous; be empathetic; be pissed off if you want; but don't be boring!

For examples of cunningly clever collection letters go to:

www.CunninglyCleverMarketing.com

Put as much effort into writing your collection letters as you do your sales letters and you'll collect money much faster!

CHAPTER 139

Getting Free Ads and Media Time

Most businesses don't consider the option of bartering with the media. Newspapers, sports teams, TV, radio, websites, and magazines of all kinds are willing to do marketing for you on trade! In fact, along with the travel business, they may be the most receptive industry in the world when it comes to leveraging their assets!

I had a huge database of US golfers but lacked a database of UK golfers so I wanted to make that one of my priorities. While I was in the UK over the summer I looked up the websites of all the major golf magazines and sent them an email suggesting a joint venture to build their databases. Although none of them knew who I was, several responded and one of the biggest agreed to a trade. I got them some free resort vacations in return for full-page ad space in their four highly-targeted publications.

The ads I will run will be full-page sweepstakes ads with over $50,000 worth of prizes — all donated by partners who want expo-sure to the UK market! Along with a follow-up email to everyone who enters, I build a huge database, my partners get access to the UK market without spending a dime, and the magazine owner gets a really nice vacation out of the rain in sunny Florida.

Win, win, win!

With my hotel and resort partners, I frequently trade for free radio, TV, banner ads, and newspaper and sports program space. I have traded websites for media space and I've traded my expertise for free media. You can do the same and get a significant amount of media without spending any cash.

Most media are very receptive to creative deals, including straight trades!

But you have to ask!

CHAPTER 140

The Complicated Way Customers Think About Your Business

In other chapters I've talked about the power of creating an experience for your customers, something that goes beyond what they normally get from a gas station, restaurant, or salon.

Something that makes them go WOW!

To further explore what you might do to heighten your customers' experience, let's look at some of the complicated ways in which customers can be subtly influenced either positively or negatively about your business.

As you read, think about the ways in which you as a customer are influenced by these factors and how they effect your opinions.

There are basically 5 key ways that a customer is influenced:

- sight
- sound
- scent
- taste
- touch

Does your business *look* high end, professional, cozy, cheap, clinical, warm, friendly, new, old, tired, futuristic, retro, or drab?

What colors do you use on your walls, floors, windows, and trucks? Cold blues, warm reds, earthy browns, hot pinks? What message do the colors you use in your business send out to your customers?

Are they "in" colors? (Look at this year's hot cars or fashions for whatever colors are hot!) Are yours hot or are they passé and telling your customers that you're behind the times?

How does your business *sound?* Does it sound silent, quiet, noisy, upbeat, dead?

Does it *smell* warm, new, moldy, stale, spicy (think Starbucks)? Is there anything for them to *taste* at your business?

What do your customers *touch* — chairs, desks, countertops? Are they plastic, metal, marble, or fur? What message does that send to your customers?

What is your customer's first impression likely to be from the total sum of all these factors?

When you think of all the things that can influence a customer positively or negatively about your business, it makes your head spin doesn't it? Spinning or not, thinking about these questions and taking some positive action on the answers could well give your business an edge in your market!

**Are you marketing your business to
all five senses to maximize your
customers' experience?**

CHAPTER 141

Selling Ferraris on eBay and the Power of the Damaging Admission

Several years ago I decided to sell my Ferrari 355 on eBay (yeah, it was red). I put up a fairly typical eBay ad that included a bunch of photos. It sold to someone in Mexico who then, surprise, surprise, did not come through with the money.

I put it up again, nothing. And again, nothing.

I had already bought another car so by the fourth listing it was time to put some real focus on selling the car. I rewrote the ad from scratch eliminating the typical BS you see in car ads and going instead for complete disclosure.

The headline read:

Ferrari 355, The Good, The Bad, and the Ugly

The good was obvious; the bad copy said things like:

Always driven in the rain. In fact, it's my only car so instead of rotting in some rich doctor's garage, mine is actually driven daily, which is why it has 50,000 miles on it and the ultimate proof that the car is sound mechanically!

Driven on the track at every club event possible and, I have to tell you, when you own this car, that's exactly what you should do so you can experience the true potential of this awesome machine.

The ugly referred to the air vents, which had in some places melted into a thick black goo (a common problem on this car).

While the Italians are fabulous with design, great with leather, and unsurpassed in their passion for cars, plastic remains something of a mystery to them. Hence the rather poor state of a couple of the air vents, which can be easily replaced.

By admitting all the car's flaws upfront in the ad and dismissing them as best I could, I built trust and removed all the major objections or fears in advance. I sold the car at once for $3000 more than I had expected to get!

You should use this tactic in all your ads, sales letters, brochures, websites, and sales presentations.

Disclosing negative issues about your product or service in advance builds trust and removes sticking points in the sales presentation.

CHAPTER 142

How to Attract Perfect Clients and Weed Out the Riffraff!

Back in the days when I taught karate for a living, Darren Willard was the most perfect client I ever had. He was a great-looking, little, nine-year-old kid with a near-perfect memory for anything you taught him. He was enthusiastic, took private lessons, and participated in all the tournaments. His parents always paid on time and they supported all the different promotional events. They referred their friends and made positive comments rather than complaints. If there were more Darren Willards around, the world would be a better place. The good news is there are, but you have to find them.

Who Is Your Perfect Client?

Can you describe the qualities of your perfect clients? You may immediately think of somebody in your business. Good, because the first step in finding better customers is to truly understand what your perfect customers should look like. What age is he or she? Is it a boy? Is it a girl? Is it a man? Is it a woman? What is their level of income? What type of job do they have? Where do they live? What do they read? Where do they work? Exactly what are your perfect customers' characteristics?

Do this exercise with your staff.

Try to come up with four or five different people who would

seem to be perfect clients. Take a look at the profile of the perfect client, because from now on that's the only type of client you want to attract!

Can you do that?

Yes, you really can. You can target-market good customers. But in order to do this, you have to know what a good customer looks like. How much money do they earn? Where do their children go to school? Where do they go to church? Where do they eat out? Which clubs do they join?

Take the time to establish profiles of your key customers. Once you have that kind of information, use it. Then you can go out with a direct-mail campaign, with a promotional campaign, with an ad campaign in a school newspaper, a church newsletter, or something similar to pinpoint and target-market these people.

You can target ONLY good customers IF you know exactly what they look like!

CHAPTER 143

The Secret to Exponential Growth for Your Company

We are not done yet but we are getting close, so it's time to tie all these cunningly-clever ideas together for you and share with you the secret to exponential growth for your company. The key to taking every element of your marketing and improving it!

Make your USP clear. Build and keep building your prospect database, then sort it into as many logical segments as you can and market one-to-one! Improve the quality of your headlines. Improve the quality of your copy. Improve the quality of your layouts for readability. Improve your calls to action and be specific! Make your offers irresistible and follow up relentlessly utilizing direct mail and email.

Provide sales scripts and training for your people, along with a solid upgrade and referral system. Last but not least, test and measure every campaign so you are constantly refining your marketing and improving your results.

Now, let's do the math.

Let's say your data collection effort nets just 3% more prospects, your headlines attract 3% more people, your copy 3% more readership, your offers 3% more response, your sales people 3% more sales and upgrades. Pretty soon your incremental marketing improvements add up to exponential growth for your business!

**Exponential growth comes from
incremental improvements at every stage of
your marketing process!**

Everything counts!

CHAPTER 144

Going Global by Following a Marketing System that Works Anywhere!

I just opened an office in the UK where we already have a number of partners up and running. How did I get partners so quickly?

Simple, I followed my normal marketing system. I built a Marketing Commander website, sent out a content-rich newsletter, and offered free special reports and audio seminars.

Then we followed up on the leads with a scripted and orchestrated sales presentation. In short, I followed my system, the same one I have used, refined, and profited from for over twenty years!

It's essential that you adopt or develop your own marketing system. Systems always produce better results. And they make it easier to repeat successful marketing.

How to Create a Strong Marketing System

1. **Establish Your Desired Results.** Each system should have a clear, concise statement of the results the system is intended to accomplish.

2. **Diagram the System.** The system should be pre-

sented in a diagram showing the sequence of events and how they relate to each other.

3. **Describe Clear Benchmarks.** Each action should be identified in sequence so that benchmarks or intermediate goals are created and the process is clear and unmistakable to anyone who will perform the work.

4. **Assign Accountability.** Accountability must be assigned for each part of the system and for the overall system. Accountability should be identified by position, not by person. People come and go — accountability does not!

5. **Determine the Timing.** Set specific timelines for each benchmark and document them.

6. **Identify Required Resources.** Every system requires resources such as staffing, postage, supplies, and information. A detailed list of the specific needed resources and quantities must be provided.

7. **Quantify the System.** How will you know you are getting the results you want? You need quantification to give you that objective view.

8. **Establish Standards.** A good system sets the standards for performance and behavior of the staff operating it. Standards are most easily stated in terms of quantity, quality, and behavior.

9. **Document the System.** It's not a system until it's documented! You cannot expect people to follow a system that is not documented.

10. **Train in System Usage.** Both management and staff must be trained in the proper use of the system *so*

that EVERY lead is handled in a seamless, consistent, and systematic manner.

Companies with marketing systems produce better results than those without!

CHAPTER 145

The Simple Secret to a Massive Increase in Sales

By now I am sure you see a great many ways by which you can improve the response to your marketing. Building a large database of prospects, segmenting your lists, developing a USP and irresistible offer, to name just a few.

But there is one more secret to getting a massive response from your marketing. The one thing that can make or break everything that has gone before: The quality, or lack thereof, of your salespeople, operators, counter staff or whoever first comes into contact with a new prospect or customer!

The person who answers the phone can make or lose you millions. Yet, despite this fact, barely one in a hundred businesses have written sales scripts, adequate sales training, and a structured sales system that moves prospects through the sales funnel in a logical and orchestrated manner.

If the person answering the phone can close one out of two calls instead of one out of four, you increase YOUR business by an astonishing 100% at a cost of almost zero!

While you can't train everyone to be a sales superstar, you can train almost anyone to be significantly better at selling! With each small improvement on how they greet, qualify, present, handle objections, and close, YOU make more money!

Lots more money!

That's why the very next book you should read is Cunningly Clever Selling! (www.CunninglyCleverSelling.com)

Before you spend a dime on marketing, make sure you have a back-end sales system in place with adequate scripting, training, and accountability in place!

This is the end of this book but not the end of your journey. **Be sure to visit the Cunningly Clever Marketing Vault for more information.** You have a free, three-month membership to the vault included with the purchase of this book!

Go to www.CunninglyCleverMarketing.com and activate your free membership now. There you will find hundreds more pages of samples, money-making tips, and marketing strategies!

I am sure that after reading this book you have conjured up some cunningly clever ideas of your own.

So what are you waiting for — get out there and test them!

And be sure to let me know how you do through our marketing forum. I'd wish you good luck, but people as clever as you seldom need it!

All the best,

Andrew Wood

Index